RECAPTURING THE TRUST

Recapturing the Trust

50 Years of Declining Trust in American Organizations and What You Can Do about it

Robert Schachat, Ph.D.

iUniverse, Inc.

New York Lincoln Shanghai

Recapturing the Trust
50 Years of Declining Trust in American Organizations and What You Can Do about it

iUniverse, Inc.

For information address:
iUniverse, Inc.
2021 Pine Lake Road, Suite 100
Lincoln, NE 68512
www.iuniverse.com

ISBN: 0-595-27882-5

Printed in the United States of America

DEDICATION

First, to my daughter, Arielle, who has been my teacher in matters of the heart and from whom I have learned about unconditional love and trust.

Second, to Shelley, Florence, and Benjamin Schachat, mother and grandparents of Arielle, whose memory lives on within us both.

Contents

Should you wish to scan this book for instant tips
and "how-tos"—specific behaviors, skills, techniques,
tools, and statements you can use to generate or recapture trust with your people, look for the "trustnet".

ACKNOWLEDGEMENTS

Thanks to all of the people who played a part in this book: those friends and colleagues who have encouraged and provoked me to action; to the people whom I interviewed and whose words I've proudly spread throughout; to the mentors and teachers upon whose shoulders I have gratefully stood in order to see the world as I do.

Thanks to the Mercy College community with its distinguished faculty and staff. Thanks also to its extraordinary student body—unmatched anywhere in its diversity and its "salt-of-the-earth pragmatism." My experience there has nurtured my work, providing me with continual support, critique, insight, and intellectual and personal renewal.

Thanks to so many of my business associates and friends who at different times loved to talk about the principles and dilemmas related to this book, giving me pause and confirmation—Rita Bigel Casher, Bill Carlin, Dan Dana, Laura Deutsch, Renee Fogarty, Jane Friedland, Jonathan Herman, Ann Ives, Ronna Kabatznick, Frank McCluskey, Stanley Moskowitz, Sandy Nathan, Larry Polsky, Bill Straubinger, Bill Wolfson and Marilyn Zavidow. Thanks toTom Hopkins, Ph.D., licensed psychologist and psychometrician, whose ability to shape a well-wrought quiz is matched only by his ability to smack a handball.

Finally, thanks to Howard Canaan, Ph.D., professor in the English and Humanities Division at Mercy College, who in the editing of the book, helped me think through, and deftly craft, a way of addressing the many intellectual and structural questions and dilemmas.

WHY THIS BOOK

As a management consultant and organizational psychologist, my job is finding creative and acceptable ways to provoke truth between people...not love or liking necessarily, just the truth when its communication is relevant to a business and business relationships. I've always been fascinated by the impact the word "trust" has in all kinds of conversation and situations. Bringing up the topic of "trust" at work inevitably evokes a variety of strong reactions. After hearing some long and convoluted complaint about a supervisor or "management," I tend to get right to the heart of the issue by asking: "Do you trust (him, her, them)?"

A long, telling pause follows. A mass of otherwise confused bundles of recriminations, emotions, and physical discomforts is settled at once with the admission that, "Well, no, I don't."

Now the real talking can begin!

How about you? Does the word "trust" provoke a strong reaction? Let's try: answer from 1 to 10 (low to high) the extent to which you trust your supervisor. Or, any one of your direct reports. Or, how about me? Here I am, after all, a stranger to most of you, and you are devoting a significant portion of your precious free time to read my ideas. Well, on a scale of 1 to 10, do you trust me enough to read on and feel that this reading experience will be a good use of your time? Do you have what it takes to trust others? Or how about yourself? To what extent do people in your organization and others in general trust you? Do you have what it takes to enable others to trust you?

This book will help you in all those human interactions where trust plays a vital part—and do you know anywhere it doesn't? It will help you consider the impact of your own attitudes about trusting others and provide tips on how to enhance productivity and satisfaction at work.

What does "trust" really mean? Why is trust such an important issue today? How is trust generated in the first place? How can it be lost? And how can it be found, once lost? How can this elusive human emotion be recaptured?

This book is about the role that trust plays in human relations, specifically in the world of work, which consumes so much of our lives. This book is also about demonstrating how trust has declined in so many American institutions, particularly in American businesses and organizations, and about some of the best practices we all can use to recapture it.

In researching and writing this book, I've become acutely aware of the vital importance of trust. Everyone I've spoken with has an opinion on the subject, and the range of responses is as varied as the backgrounds of the people consulted. My own opinions were confirmed as I found myself emotionally moved by people who have suffered from what they would describe as a lifetime of lost and, in some cases, never experienced, trust at work. Many of my conversations traveled to examples of personal, non-work situations, reflecting many of the same causes and effects.

But to get a handle on this admittedly broad subject and because this topic is the center of my consulting services, I have narrowed the topic to <u>organizational trust</u>. And while I examine a wide variety of circumstances involving trust, I focus ultimately on what leaders—employers, managers, supervisors and mentors—can do and say to recapture trust among employees.

I've included an autobiographical chapter, in part to help further define how I see trust and in part to introduce you to and interest you in, some of the kinds of experiences which made the pursuit of human connectedness a delightful lifelong journey for me.

This book is also about what you can do to recapture the trust: as a friend, colleague, or as anyone who wishes to influence the quality of worklife in your organization.

In my twenty years of college teaching, twenty-five years working with leaders of developing countries, and thirty years of organizational training and counseling in over one hundred fifty organizations, I've gathered a wide range of data from surveys, focus groups, class discussions, and individual interviews on the subject of trust.

As a human relations-oriented organizational psychologist and management consultant, I've been particularly sensitive to negative, hurtful, and counterproductive behaviors in the world of work. We don't have to watch *Death of a Salesman*, *Working Woman*, or *Nine to Five* to be reminded of the abrasive and abusive conduct that occurs in too many of our organizations. Now, with sexual harassment legal suits that extend to all sorts of "hostile environment" criteria, these issues are surfacing more than ever. Damaging emotional experiences are generating other serious side effects, and many experts are looking into the relationship between workplace violence and stressful and humiliating working conditions.

Clearly, such gross and obvious abuse contributes to worker mistrust and alienation. But, there are subtle behaviors that do not constitute an overt "hostile" environment, yet are equally destructive to productivity and employee satisfaction. Interpersonal insensitivities such as snubbing and put-downs, blaming, secretive decision-making, withholding valuable information, sarcasm, deception, arrogance, and threats all erode trust. And trust can be compromised by perceptions related to a betrayal of written or implied agreements.

Sadly, many of these behaviors are tacitly accepted because they are an unfortunate all-too-common norm of human interaction, especially in stressful business environments. These behaviors are so much the norm, that they have too often become unconsciously accepted as "life at work." It's disheartening to see how many people accept abuse of power and emotional isolation as a "given" of organizational life!

For a variety of complex reasons, organizations breed suspicions and suspiciousness.

A cycle of suspicion occurs: management questions an employee's trustworthiness and micromanages that person, who, resenting the micromanagement, behaves in a way that arouses additional suspiciousness!

What do you think a recent sample of graduating high school seniors gave as their overwhelming choice of preferred management strategies (assuming that they were the managers): authoritarian, democratic/ participatory, or permissive? The answer: authoritarian. Why? Most said that they wouldn't trust their workers…especially their peers, with whom they had just spent years trying to outwit authorities at school. So the problem of mistrust at work starts long before the first day on the job.

The simple danger is this: If we don't break this cycle of mistrust, we'll all continue to suffer from the effects of low-trusting environments.

The effect of a low-trust work environment is clear and evident: it is unhealthy for humans and profits! Low trust in the workplace yields low morale and low creativity. Extensive research over the years has concluded that these conditions are deadly for the bottom-line as well.

Still another troubling aspect of low-trust environments is how they affect people's general spirit. What we read and hear about "anger and violence in the workplace" and "people not finding meaning in their lives" is, in part, due to the problem of trust at work. We are, after all, highly social animals, and much of our spirit comes from our healthy relationships with others and groups of others.

How long does a spirit—even a young and fresh one—hold on before being burnt out by an unhealthy and non-supportive environment? I'm delighted to assert that there is hope. Dysfunctional and trust-eroding behaviors, unconscious and normative though they may have become, are responsive to simple trust-building cures outlined throughout this book. These are identified by "trustnet" icons which have been included as reference guides.

The Fragility of Trust

Trust is like a butterfly, capricious and delicate. To capture a butterfly, one has to use a soft net and a gentle touch.

Throughout this book and specifically in Chapter Four, I'll present practices we can all use to recapture the trust. I use the word "recapture" quite deliberately. "Fooled once, shame on you; fooled twice, shame on me," is an all-too-common expression, suggesting the precarious, elusive and skittish nature of trust. Once lost, trust is not quickly rebuilt. For many with whom I've spoken, betrayal of trust is never forgotten nor forgiven. Determinants such as social norms, personality types, personal histories, and reward systems affect our sensitivity to issues of trust. People's propensity to trust varies as greatly as opinions and temperament; yet even among the most naively trusting of us, once a breach of trust is noticed, trust is slow to come back.

For many, trust grows slowly—even in the safest of situations.

There is a passage in The *Little Prince*, written by Antoine de Saint Exupéry, that captures this sense of the fragility involved in establishing trust. The fox is explaining how the Prince must treat him in order to be friends:

"I cannot play with you," the fox said. "I am not tamed." "What does that mean—'tame ?'" asked the boy. The fox re-plied, "As of now, you are like any of the thousands of boys I see. If you wish to play with me, you must tame me. If you tame me, we shall need each other, and, to me, you will be unique in all the world…You must be patient. First you will sit down at a little distance from me…I shall look at you out of the corner of my eye…then you will sit closer every day."

When trust escapes, we become detached from others and our-selves. We don't relate emotionally or intellectually. Alienation results from this disconnection between people. When people are distrustful of one another, they display distinct symptoms:

- Talking at and not with one another.

- Conveying only thoughts and opinions, never reactions or feelings.

- Ignoring the impact of what they say or do on another's self-esteem.

- Treating others as objects to serve a specific purpose.

- Playing interpersonal poker by maintaining facades and im-ages—instead of revealing the feelings they may harbor behind the statements they make.

Sound familiar? I'm sure it does. "lack of communication," "lack of commitment," "lack of teamwork," "lack of leadership," or "lack of vision," are among the most often uttered laments of the thousands of clients I've worked with over the last thirty years in the consulting business. The underlying issue always turns out be a lack of trust. And, when examined, the associated emotion is a sense of lonely distance and emptiness.

Recapturing the Trust

But I believe there is an antidote to this condition—a key to recapturing the trust. That antidote is authenticity. Authenticity implies "truth"—an honesty between people that can be seen and heard in word and in deed. In business, one's word is essential. Whether a person's word is doubted because of purposeful deception or an interpersonal failing in trying to match one's good intent to the perceived behavior, the effect is the same: distrust due to a perceived betrayal of one's word.

We all know that authenticity—interpersonal honesty and integrity—is difficult to achieve and maintain in our increasingly suspicious world, especially in our more competitive environments, many of which actively promote negativity and distrust. This is not to be confused with "naive openness or self-disclosure." (In competitive work environments, a lot of personal information is better left unsaid.) Authenticity involves the ability to courageously encounter others: to be "present" and "in the moment" to them so that they know they are visible and have an impact on you. Authenticity requires that one can encounter another squarely and face-to-face, and get down to what's really going on between them, with no pretense, no facades, no BS.

Tell someone how you really feel about him or her with respect, and you have gone a long way towards a trusting friendship.

For most people authenticity is very difficult. Most people have never been taught or had role models from whom to learn.

And, because most people are unfamiliar with this skill and its benefits, authenticity feels threatening and counterproductive.

"Why would I ever want to tell someone I work with how I really feel about them?" is the all-too-common response to my never-ending plea to "tell the truth about how you feel with any and all close work associates."

Of course you need to have two skills: first, to say it so that others can "hear" it, and second, to know when and when not to say it.

The work I offer in this book will not be easy, but the rewards are incalculably high.

In my own way, I strive for authenticity by speaking the truth, that is, by expressing what I see and feel about the behavior of others and acting in a way that helps others do the same with me. In professional terms, I help organizations and individuals within organizations achieve the multiple gifts of authenticity—gifts not only of personal joy and aliveness, but also of productivity and world-class excellence. Without authenticity, there is a spiritual death between people, a "death-in-life," as Coleridge might have put it. We have a choice in life. Remember the dice players, "Death" and "Death-in-Life" who gambled for the souls of the Ancient Mariner's shipmates? The winner was "Death-in-Life," and the mariners had to endure a soulless and non-contactful life, a fate worse than death.

This does not have to be your fate.

Don't get me wrong; I'm no saint. My reality, like that of most people I know and have known, is far less tranquil, less emotionally riveting and contactful than it could be. While I love and long to disclose the truth, keep my word, and push the boundaries as much as existing norms and my own inhibitions will allow, I too often follow the drab norms of acceptable behavior and say things diplomatically so as to soften my real intent. Most people do the same with me, and together we dance a dispirited waltz through life.

Most of us struggle with trusting others. We criticize ourselves and others and burn when people don't live up to our standards, especially if that undesirable behavior interferes with our wants and needs. I have my favorite list of people whom, because I don't like their behavior, I have difficulty trusting. Their characteristics are: arrogance, bragging, bullying, controlling, hypocrisy, ignorance, refusing to take feedback, know-it-allness, officiousness, sarcasm, self-centeredness, and snobbery. But who among us doesn't act in these ways at times? Did you ever catch yourself complaining to someone, "I'm the only person who is considerate, or honest, or knows what to do, or is rational around here"? But, come on, we're all human. Our task is to keep working on the skills that build liking, respect, and trust. Being open to giving and receiving feedback about the helpful and the non-helpful things we say and do are the skills of authenticity that will help us and those with whom we interact.

This book is about those skills and about the benefits gained from using them; and about how to bring out the best in others so as to strengthen good will and trust, and, as a result, increase profits.

Many people have rarely experienced the directness and the honesty described in this book—especially at work, and they don't believe they can foster trusting, authentic, and supportive relationships in competitive work situations.

I know they can!

My persistent optimism comes from having witnessed profound insight and change in my students and clients over the years. I have seen significant attitude and behavioral change when people become familiar with the mechanics and the experience of human relations. And, they invariably become more satisfied and successful.

While authentic relationships do not take any more time than manipulative ones, there is an illusion that they do. A common resistance to, and distraction from, trust and relationship building is the obsessive quality and the frenzy of many people's lives. Some people who are not trusted or trusting are simply caught up in a fear-induced success syndrome characterized by a time urgency and an obsession for winning and material acquisition. They insist that they have little time or inclination for tranquil or reflective interpersonal moments. "Inside," many people assert, they are decent people—but it does take work to get "inside."

I trust the human heart. While I'm no stranger to tragedy and the capricious unfairness of life, I know as well the underlying human spirit and its wish to love and be loved. I've seen this so many times—even among the hardest of hearts—that I know it is true! This awareness has reaffirmed my trust, again and again. And, while my work life's purpose sometimes takes two steps back for every one I achieve, I have learned to cherish all those steps forward.

So why continue reading?

- If you are a supervisor or manager, wishing to learn more about how to generate trust among your employees…

- If you are the head of any business division coping with the challenges of attracting and retaining the talent you need to grow your bottom line…

- If you are new to the world of work, wondering about what to expect today and tomorrow and wish to make a difference…

- If you spend a lot of time at work and wish to have work be a life-enhancing experience that promotes your personal growth and spirit and fulfills your need for meaning and community and wish to recapture a trust of your own…

Keep reading.

1
MY PERSONAL ODYSSEY

So, how did I get this obsession with "trust?"

This chapter is about the demographics and events of my life that shaped my take on the condition of trust and on those factors that led to the decline of trust in American institutions.

And who's telling this story?

I'm a business professor, a management consultant, and a once-and-always social psychologist.

My doctoral training was long on scientific rigor and methodology, complete with professional objectivity and neutrality regarding the phenomena being examined.

But forgive me; this book is not written with the objectivity and epistemological humility of a scientist. It is written from my experience, passions, and values.

This is my story seen through my filters.

Consequently, this book is also written by a person whose view has been affected by yet another combination of filters: those of a baby boomer, son, student, actor, traveler, and father.

I confess that I am both enthralled by and partially blind to the short-comings of my own "babyboomer youth generation," weaned as we were on hopes of utopia and ever ready to champion a cause or a high calling. While I may in fact have been part of the dreaded "establishment" these last thirty years, I have nevertheless considered myself to be among those who have held on to other hopes.

I watched my generation fall heavily from its spiritual peak, as the assassinations of the late 'sixties, coupled with the Vietnam War, began to weaken our confidence. Watergate-driven cynicism and the reces-sion-fueled 'seventies further disillusioned us. By the early 'seventies, social and economic conditions could no longer nurture a countercul-ture. The 'eighties brought the "me" generation, Reaganomics, and the yuppie phenomenon. The 'nineties has produced a population intoxi-cated with technology and materialism, spending three fourths of its life at work, and consisting of people bent upon acquiring the good life while the getting is good, yet underneath wishing for time to savor the sparkle of the morning dew, feel the pleasures of body and spirit, and yield to their own embedded sorrows and the sorrows of their fellow human beings.

My early perceptions and social commentary of the world began, as with most people, with my observations of other kids and families. Such variety in kids! How could they be so different from my sister and me? How could they embrace the things we would sneer at and sneer at the things we would embrace? And the families they belonged to, how varied and strange they were! How bizarre were some of these kids, par-ents, pets, and home decors…some kids never combed their hair; some parents included their kids in family discussions, treating them as adults; some let their dogs eat from their plates and lick their mouths (yech!); and some had lime-green velvet sofas protected by thick stick-to-the-seat-of-your-pants plastic. And what if one or, heaven forbid, both parents were in the mental health field? Everyone in those days knew that a psychologist's kid was always a kook.

So my home was normal—like yours, right? It took a while to come to the realization that the norms of my family were not necessarily the healthiest and best, as we were innocently led to believe.

My family dynamic shaped my early formulations of what was right and wrong, good and bad, moral and immoral. Other influences included a combination of my extended family, my friends and their families, my community, and the communities I've come in contact with during my life. And certain formative experiences with these communities have helped shape who I am and what I believe. What follows are eight life experiences that are among the most profound memories of my life. These experiences are all bound with lessons in human nature, particularly as it relates to trust. Here, in chronological order are these life-defining moments that led to this calling and to this book.

THE COMFORTS OF HOME

Like most kids, I liked the comfort of being at home. No one went to nursery schools when I was growing up in the 'fifties, and the concept of day-care center was still twenty or so years away. No, I, like all the other kids my age, stayed at home, literally and figuratively holding on to my mommy's apron strings. My mother doted on me and worried about every sniffle, lest a hay fever-induced sneeze blossom into some dreaded illness. My father was a serious teetotaler, and, in keeping with his generational cohorts, rather remote, preferring to have a provider role within the family and leave the nurturing to the Dr. Spock-inspired stay-at-home mom. Seemingly always in suit and tie, he whisked daily along the Long Island Rail Road to Penn Station, the clearinghouse of all the New York City Dashing Dan 'fifties-style "organization men." Add an older sister to whom every breath I took was an annoyance, and you have a rather typical mid-century suburban family situation, complete with about an average amount of what was called nagging then, emotional abuse today, leading to about an average amount of neurotic acting out.

My house was warm. I enjoyed staring out my den window, leaning against the back of an oh-so-comfortable sofa, the radiator providing just enough heat to balance the chill emanating from the frost-cooled window. I would stare outside this window, aware of the protection about me, and daydream of times gone by. I vaguely remember associating that feeling of warmth with a feeling of absolute comfort and security in a baby carriage, my face lightly chilled, while I was tucked under several woolen blankets. What more could a young mind with so little experience know as trust but the presence of warmth, protection, and safety? I was fortunate enough to have been given this sense of trust and comfort as a child.

MEMORIES FROM
A KINDER KINDERGARTEN

My first weeks at kindergarten were unsettling for me. I remember not wanting to go. I remember my father trying to bribe me with a ten dollar bill, a distraction that lasted but a few moments. I knew I didn't want to go, but I knew that I had no choice. I remember the half-formed idea in my mind that there was some overwhelmingly strong reason for a child to go to school. But I also remember being in class and not wanting to participate in any class activity. The class seemed cold and austere. Miss Shepard, my kindergarten teacher, may have been cordial enough, but she seemed distant; she didn't have my mother's special warmth. I never felt the warmth of her touch; her eyes never engaged mine to lessen their troubled intensity.

I remember my anxiety, sitting in some circle while Miss Shepard read us a book and panned the illustrations so that we could all see, as I sat uneasily, planning my escape. I remember a classmate wondering aloud why I was crying. I remember a fire drill that allowed me my escape to the parking lot, where I hoped my mother would be. I remember being restrained and pulled back to class.

But this story had a quick and happy ending, for I also remember a cherished personal gift: After I was brought back tearful to class, Mr. Reynolds, the school vice principal, promised to and indeed did walk with me every day during lunch, just to be with me and chat with me. Within days I was converted, not necessarily into a good little student—I was always a little too restive and dreamy for that distinction—but I now felt safe. I had the contact I so desperately needed. How honored and flattered and soothed I, a little five-year-old, was made to feel! Maybe I needed more one-on-one attention than the average kid. Maybe I was a little more anxious and a little less trusting. But it didn't take much. We couldn't have had more than two or three walks together, but that my feelings of dread were dissolved. I now felt safe, connected, and trusting.

Kindergarten was, of course, my first foray into the world outside of my very protective home, my first encounter with an institutional organization. Like most encounters with institutions, it had its stresses and compensations. But as a first start, it gave me something emotionally that has stayed with me. While I may have forgotten almost every other event of those early years, I have not forgotten that unusually profound trusting relationship developed in me at such a tender age at one meeting, which put me at peace and confirmed my trust. Perhaps this early first encounter with an organization's human touch shaped in me a life-long sensitivity to organizational relationships. It has certainly made me understand and appreciate at first hand the importance of a "Mr. Reynolds," of a caring presence, everywhere, but especially in otherwise anonymous organizations.

Be a Mr. Reynolds for every newcomer in your group. Offer your mentorship, support, and understanding.

THE THEATER CONNECTION
AND ITS CORE OF TRUST

Think what you may about the world of actors and the theater, there's no better place to savor one's flesh and soul than in the art of acting, of portraying human connectedness.

Ever since my sixth-grade performance as U.S. Grant in *Alice in April Land*, I've loved the stage, where I could luxuriate in a world of relationships at their most raw and intimate, free from the restrictive emotional norms so often filtering the real feelings between people. What a release to have a place to express my feelings, to be rewarded, not punished, for speaking the unspeakable! The euphoria I felt upon reaching my character and achieving the truth with a scene-partner taught me that one avenue to joy lies in profound connection. The intimacy of knowing who you really are, shameful feelings and all, and of sharing that glorious authenticity is a unique payoff of stage acting.

While the portrayal of a character may be the words and actions of another, the gift to both the actor and the audience is that the relationships and feelings exchanged and, when written and portrayed well, are universal. I've never been a servant to a queen, but having played the oily servant Oswald in *King Lear*, I sure know what it's like to experience simultaneously the feelings of intimidation and steadfast loyalty. I've never been a soldier in jail about to be shot, but as the condemned prisoner in Brendan Behan's *The Hostage*, I knew all too well the feelings of being misunderstood and panicky. Of course I've never actually been a rat, but having gained the character of Bobby Rat (first name similarity just coincidental) in Israel Horowitz's *Rats*, I know the anguish of being confronted with the prospect of unattainable success: impenetrable garbage cans! The miracle of theater enables us, as actors and as audiences, to experience authentic emotions in fictional situations.

Psychologically also, drama is a vehicle for truth. A playwright weaves a tale unfolding the authentic motivations surrounding relationships, while the director and the actors toil to manifest those motivations to ensure that the audience both appreciates the performance and fully comprehends and emotionally experiences and integrates the message.

While literature contains many profound statements about human failings and nobility, no other literary genre focuses so exclusively on human relationships as drama. Its primary medium is human conversation, either with another, within a group, or alone with the audience...but always to the audience. Actors always share feelings with an audience, whose members derive pleasure from an emotional intimacy, not only with the character (or characters) on stage, but with themselves. As we, the audience, experience theater, we eavesdrop on the excruciatingly private world of others while connecting at some level with the thoughts and actions of each player. The experience of an uninterrupted two-to-three-hour play is a visit to a rarely viewed place within oneself. What a remarkable and liberating experience! Great comedy will lighten anyone's mood. Perhaps it will even heal physical illness, as Norman Cousins and Patch Adams promise. And great tragedy heals the heart.

In his *Poetics*, Aristotle calls the healing power of great tragedy *catharsis*. Aristotle finds a pattern of redemption in a great tragedy like Sophocles's *Oedipus Rex*. He describes the hero's tragic flaw, the refusal to see the life-threatening psychic demons within himself, and the succession of events that ultimately breaks this denial. Then, a *peripitea*, the reversal of events leads to the hero's fall, and *anagnorosis*, the recognition of the true nature of his being, fills the hero with an epiphanic awareness at the end. And while the tragic hero or heroine travels through this hellish journey culminating in a state of knowing grace, the audience watches in pity and fear. We identify with the underlying (if not the very same) flaws, denials, downfall, and knowing grace and revel in the light of catharsis. This is the letting-go process, the opening to emotions, the shedding of defenses and facades and the euphoria of surrender, which the early Greek philosopher/psychologist playwrights knew to be essential to the human condition.

We, as audience, connect to those powerful human emotions. We know and feel the pain of our own lives simultaneously. For most of us live in denial of our feelings as well, yet most of us also have known the bittersweet surrender to our truth. It was this soulful connection between actor and actor, and between audience and actor, that helped to reawaken my connection to my fellow human beings. The emotional language of the theater can help us recapture our trust in one another.

Let yourself feel your emotions for yourself and the character, in this extraordinary moment from the movie version of *Brigadoon*. Gene Kelly is beginning to believe he may, in fact, be in some kind of enchanted time and space warp when he asks the kindly leader to describe what it's like to go to sleep for one hundred years to escape the treacheries of the world. This lovable and caring old man responds in a Scottish brogue and expresses the following sentiment:

> It's like being carried on shadowy arms to a distant cloud. And there I float. Yet sometimes, I think I hear strange voices. They say no words that I can remember, yet their voices are filled with a fearful longing. It's as if...there are millions of people crying out in pain. My goodness...(He turns to Gene Kelly, misty-eyed.) There must be a woeful amount of sorrow in the outside world.

I know of no one who has been spared a full measure of sorrow in his or her life. Remember that people connect deeply and trust when sorrow is shared and acknowledged. Encourage such expression. The cathartic release, along with human connectedness, frees the individual for more focus, creativity, and collaboration.

¿HABLA USTED ESPAÑOL?

As part of my fascination with relationships, I chose foreign languages as a college major because they immersed me in the mind and culture of others far different from me. What better way to walk in the moccasins of another than to speak in his or her tongue? Speaking Spanish, for example, tends to bring out my more poetic, musical, and romantic side. I lived with a family in Guadalajara, Mexico, during part of my sophomore year in college. How I remember the wonderful effects of many of their cultural norms: the pace of living arranged so that experiences could be savored, the glorious afternoon siestas (I would read a chapter or two of a novel each day to bring on a dream-filled sleep). And there was live music everywhere!

Speaking Spanish has led to new personal and business opportunities as well. I've conducted seminars throughout Latin and South America and have been able to know its people and culture far more intimately than if I were a tourist relying on third-party translations.

This interest in cultural diversity led me to a long-term relationship with the United Nations-sponsored Center for International Community Health Services, where I have been training government employees from throughout the developing world in management and leadership, for going on twenty-six years. Because I facilitate training in human relations, trust and team building, the discussions are unusually intimate, and I've shared deepest thoughts and feelings with people as different from me as can be found on Earth. This experience has opened me up not only to human differences, but to human sameness as well.

These government employees I've trained have lived amidst unspeakable horrors that most of us in the U.S. know about only through the aesthetic distance of the media. Few of us have witnessed the brutality and havoc wrought by both natural and "unnatural" (human) forces. In the last few years, for example, many of our participants have been from Rwanda and other sub-Saharan African countries that have been devastated by continuous civil and border wars and drought-induced famine.

I've observed how countless initiatives among these countries' leaders to manage public service have repeatedly crashed. I often ask the new officials about the whereabouts and fortunes of their previous counterparts, and when the news is a dismal commentary of human politics at its worst, we both shake off our frustration and start a new initiative once again. For these dedicated people, tomorrow is another day, and, like Sisyphus, they have to roll the rock up the mountain again, finding meaning and identity through their work. And, maybe tomorrow things will change.

What a lesson in the resilience of the human spirit I've learned from these people! What undying optimism they share with the people on whose behalf they work so tirelessly! From them, I've acquired additional faith and trust in the nature of interpersonal and community relations. Despite our differences, despite the assaults to their trust in their "fellow man," each time I meet with them, I am awed by their relentless optimism.

How alike we all are! For every one of these international dignitaries, trust is the single most critical factor affecting the success of their ventures and the emotional quality of their lives. I've found that trust and other issues involving human relations and human institutions are remarkably similar the world over. These experiences with students from at least fifty countries representing every continent and every major religion have let me see and feel the inescapable importance of achieving diversity.

Be a champion of diversity in your organization. Acclaim how you benefit from diverse thinking. Demonstrate your belief in the statement, "I value you because of our differences, not in spite of them."

CHOOSING SOCIAL PSYCHOLOGY: THE SOCIAL SCIENCE OF HUMAN NATURE

After college, my continuing fascination with human relationships led me to the field of psychology in graduate school. At first, I was attracted to Clinical Psychology, that area involved in studying and healing abnormal and dysfunctional behavior. After a sampling of graduate courses, however, I became deeply attracted to Social Psychology. How we Social Psychology students would smugly make fun of all the other psychology students! We saw the clinical psychology students as pseudosophisticated and uptight, the experimental and physiological psychology students as geeky and anti-social. Social Psychology seemed perfect for us extroverted hipsters, politically and socially astute, with but a dash of defensive self-importance.

Social psychology is the psychology of human behavior in everyday life. It explores the effects of culture and norms on human behavior, the psychology of communication, obedience to authority, persuasion, love, hate; group dynamics, the psychology of community and the psychology of community breakdown—violence, separatism, racism, ethnic and religious intolerance, and war. And at the center of all of these relationships is the complex concept of <u>trust</u>. Being in the company of social psychologists these last thirty years has meant not only being a member of a grand mutual-admiration society, but experiencing a continual reinforcement of the theoretical underpinnings of the delicate condition of trust in the various and changing human arenas.

In 1971, while at the University of Connecticut Graduate School, I had my first opportunity to discover how social psychology could be applied as a trust-building tool in organizational settings. It was there that I met psychologist-turnedmanagement consultant, Hal Kelner. Hal was a National Train-ing Laboratories staff member on contract with U Conn. He was conducting an Organizational Development program with a cross-section of individuals from the college, including myself, who wished to become an internal cadre of conflict mediators who would help settle disputes among the various constituencies of the college community.

Hal wore black and had a style that said, "Regardless of all the credit and adulation you may be mistakenly directing at me, I will nevertheless, see you as an equal in every way…and, by the way, I'm not intimidated by your position, bluster, or outrage." How I marveled at this live hero who used the genteel weapon of searing and gutsy, yet supportively honest communications! Hal Kelner's training group was my initial passage into the world of the social psychologist turned "change agent." It was the practical application of my Social Psychology learning to the outside world, using interpersonal relations and group dynamics to facilitate necessary and desired change.

And the most significant skill that we as social psychologists/change agents needed to develop was, again, facilitating trust.

In 1975 I met and worked with Gordon Lippitt, one of the most recognized of the early change agents. He was best known for his role in creating the famous study comparing three different approaches to productive management: "authoritarian," "demo-cratic," and "laissez-faire." Naturally, this study, conducted in the USA, resulted in the "democratic" style winning. In fact, all the great studies show this "democratic/participatory" approach is best, even though it is rarely practiced.

I served as a Vice President in Gordon's management consulting firm for five years. He has been quoted and cited for his hundreds of articles, books, and speeches, but a poem he read on many of his appearances captures my feelings about the problem of trust and authenticity in our institutions, a problem that was recognized even then, in the early nineteen-seventies:

If this is not a place where tears are understood, where do I go to cry?

If this is not a place where my spirit can take wing, where do I go to fly?

If this is not a place where my questions can be asked, where do I go to seek?

If this is not a place where my feelings can be heard, where do I go to speak?

If this is not a place where I can try, and learn, and grow, where can I just be me?

If this is not a place where tears are understood, where do I go to cry?

Among the many pleasures I get from my work is the opportunity to visit many "corporate cultures." Like a cultural anthropologist, I have loved observing the "natives" of over one hundred fifty organizations and noting the gross and subtle similarities and differences among them. For those of you who have lived in several, you know how some could be defined as "primitive" and others as "evolved." One thing most have in common, however, is a norm preferring what is usually described as "rational and unemotional communications." Human beings, however, are emotional beings, and emotions are always involved. With sanctions against the discussion of feelings, emotions tend to be "acted out," which is damaging to relationships. Instead of telling someone you are disappointed in his or her performance, it is more acceptable (and, by the way, destructive) to scold that person with a menacing expression and voice.

Much of my work involves the gathering of two or more parties at some off-site in order to plan their goals and roles, but also, and more importantly, to settle their current differences and conflicts. These conflict mediation meetings and retreats have taught me that the softer, more vulnerable feelings need to be recognized and nurtured, not only in our personal lives, but also in our institutional environments. Corporations in America and throughout the world tend to practice, value and reinforce rather hardheaded, logical, and practical ways of thinking and behaving.

While "Keep feelings out of the discussion" might be the most common advice given in problem solving and conflict management, the converse is the real answer: people, as well as organizations, everywhere must keep feelings in the conversation so that the real underlying issues can surface and get resolved. Once feelings are expressed and both sides feel heard and understood, the collaboration is easy!

THE HIPPIE EXPERIENCE
AND THE ART OF UNCONDITIONAL LOVE

I'm well aware of the generally negative feelings associated with the concept of "hippie." The word brings up a quick, revealing non-verbal response in almost everyone due to their particular relationship with hippies and their stand on a host of moral/ethical and political issues surrounding the then "counterculture." I recently talked with Theodore Roszak, whose 1971 book, *The Making of a Counter Culture*, best explained and defined this unique generation. He wished me a skeptical "good luck" in response to my efforts at writing this book as a means to further my wish to humanize and bring trust back into the American workplace.

My first encounter with a "hippie" was absolutely enchanting and would characterize my response to how I saw the hippie phenomenon.

When the doorbell rang, I opened the door prepared to have a friend's buddy "crash" at my apartment. I had never realized until that moment that, in our culture, men have a subtle way of checking each other out. Unsure and untrusting, we men tend to reveal of ourselves only what another male will acknowledge as male, strong, and competent/successful. It was only then, because the person standing before me didn't display such male posturing, that I became aware of this customary male-male behavior.

Instead, this fellow gazed at me and smiled. I felt an instant liking for him…not the liking you feel after you've made some critical assessments, but a liking based on no preassumptions or prejudgments…nothing. I quickly forgave his odd and unkempt-looking presentation and found myself lost in time in his presence. We talked for hours, made dinner together, and spoke about everything relevant at the time: the Vietnam War, politics, hair, the hippie subculture, happenings. This hippie simply made me feel so loved, so adequate, and without my having to prove anything to him. He had mastered the art of unconditional love.

Imagine a community based on the shared belief that spiritual connection transcends material possession. To make it in this community, status or money were irrelevant. Just being available to connect and to be present was all that mattered.

I had to experience more of this hippie stuff, up close and personal. So in the summer of 1970, I took a Route-66-like journey across America. With Two friends, Ratzo (named after the Dustin Hoffman character in *Midnight Cowboy*) and Jonny Herman, I packed my Cutlass and headed west. Ratzo had a Buster-Brown-type Beatles wig-style haircut, I had a mane of curly hair and a beard, and Jonny had a halo of sandy ringlets. We donned our bell-bottoms and t-shirts with hippie symbols, and wore something dangling around our necks and/or from our belts.

Our first stop was a memorial park somewhere in western Pennsylvania. We looked for a cool spot and found one near a fountain surrounded by some great oaks. Sitting beside the fountain were scores of hippies! In those days, they were unmistakable; they looked like us!

During that summer, we drifted from one hippie commune to another across the country, swapping stories and talking of politics and the "soft revolution" which we all coveted so.

Being a bit on the hypochondriacal side, I shared in spirit but didn't ingest the hallucinatory compounds that provided what were described as the fabulous mystical journeys that many hippies experienced. It didn't matter if I were "tripping" or not. I found that by adjusting my mind in a certain way, I could talk about the sensuality of the grass, the glorious colors of the trees, the likely thoughts of animals, the possibility of utopia; or savor the high of looking deeply into another's eyes and revealing my thoughts of the moment.

For that one brief shining moment, lasting, say, a couple of years, there was a camaraderie, an instant trust within this hippie subculture. Nearly everyone we met was like the "stranger at my door." Imagine the comfort, the delight, and the cozy warmth that I felt...like those childhood woolen blankets on a brisk winter's day.

I was convinced then, and remain convinced, of the possibility for trust in my own community, in the guy next door, the shopkeeper, or even the next person turning the corner coming my way. Trusting that one could engage a stranger without fear was one of the greatest legacies of the 'sixties generation. One of our greatest losses is the constellation of freedoms denied because of the era of distrust that followed. Locking doors, forbidding one's children to talk to strangers, the boom in personal and home security systems, and litigation madness are some of the symptoms of how we've regressed, spiritually and emotionally. For those of us who saw the possibility of the human community, these present conditions are both disheartening and motivating.

Yes, I protect and defend my belongings and loved ones, but because I also know this potential between strangers, I am eager to respond to the slightest encouragement to lower my defenses. And, due in part to what I have learned from my experiences in "face-to-face communications laboratories," I have learned how to redefine vulnerability so as to be more open and minimize my less rational suspiciousness. But more about that later...

Look for ways in which you can recreate the positive aspects of the trusting subculture of the hippies in your organization. By your own policies and behaviors, encourage your people to trust first and suspect second.

DAYS OF TM AND ROSES:
SEARCHING FOR
THE ECSTASY OF HIGHER CONSCIOUSNESS

One summer's afternoon in the late 'sixties, I was hiking along St. Mark's Place in Greenwich Village, New York City. I drifted lazily from one freak shop to another and into some bizarre-looking (even by those days' standards) clothing establishment. A guy named Bill approached me and, along with showing me some of the latest freakish wear, looked at me deeply and revealed that I appeared to be someone who was a searcher. "How did you know that?" I asked, flattered and blushing in the glow of feeling so wonderfully transparent and at being singled out as someone who was a searcher. "Oh," he said, "I can tell when I'm in the presence of one."

OK, it was the 'sixties, so I sampled a few crazy cults. They all seemed innocent enough at the time. The group of Bill's that I joined was "Nichiren Shoshu." My father couldn't stand the sound of my chanting their mantra, "Nam Yaho Renge Kyo," in my room. I chanted this phrase aloud for a half-hour at a time while rubbing a handful of stringed beads. It felt great! The constant chanting provided some sort of brain change that was quite pleasant. The meetings were real cool, too. We'd meet at this swanky building on Sutton Place in Manhattan's fashionable upper East Side, enter a large apartment with scores of shoes placed just outside its door, sit on pillows on the floor, respond to the gong drummed by a monk, and proceed, in unison, to chant the mysterious phrase over and over again until the air was filled with words that felt like tonal vibrations caressing my whole body. The sounds took me far from my everyday thoughts (an assortment of frets, longings and regrets) and replaced them with light physical sensations that triggered delightful memories. I felt light, warm, cozy again. I had recurrent images of being in that baby carriage on a cold day, wrapped in warm, soft cashmere woolen blankets. Far out!

For about a month, I grooved on this high, until I heard a rumor from a few insiders that this Buddhist group was a sect known to be a front for a fascist political party in Japan and that the chanting was intended to hypnotize us into becoming slaves to the cult. Whether the rumor was true or not, this particular brand of exploring the current craze for the spiritual world was a bit too weird for me; so off I went to seek my spiritual ecstasy elsewhere.

TM (transcendental meditation) was in the air. The Beatles did TM, Mia Farrow did TM, and Donovan, the singer, did TM. So did my friends Justin and David, so I was gonna do TM too.

It was 1972. I was in graduate school, and everybody was chanting something. I paid seventy-five dollars, got a secret word, attended seven straight evenings of "checking classes" to make sure I "thought" my two-syllable mantra (a sacred word never to be uttered aloud) correctly in my head. Twenty minutes, twice a day, at dawn and dusk, I repeated the mantra over and over again, eliminating all thought so that most of that meditation time would be spent "transcending"—being suspended in "thoughtlessness." This induced altered state of consciousness combines what is physiologically described as alpha and theta brain rhythms and is associated with a nearly impossible-to-describe state that is neither sleep, alertness, nor dream. In this trance-like state, according to the Maharishi Mahesh Yogi, one is detached from the world of relative thinking where there is good and bad, and experiences cosmic consciousness, an "absolute" state where all thoughts (sensations, emotions, memories, etc.) are good and beautiful.

For me, this practice kept its promise. I was already suspicious of spiritual cults, and I felt good being able to meditate without feeling I had to join some group and possibly get hooked in. So I meditated dawn and dusk for ten years and loved it. I guess the practice may have made me more relaxed and more spiritual. I believed that while suspended in this somnambulist state, along with the sensations of sheer joy, my "self," or awareness center, was independent of my body; I had a sensation that convinced me (at the time anyway) that my body was independent of this mind that I witnessed as a "separate entity" and, consequently it seemed that my mind would never die. Beat that for a selling point!

Meditating has deepened my understanding and belief that joy and pleasure is a here-and-now bodily feeling, achieved by turning off the judging mind and allowing one to simply experience the sensations and emotions that flow through the body—generally unnoticed—and rarely savored for the joy that they can bring (this parallels the non-critical enjoyment of another seen in the face-to-face communications laboratories). But most meditational disciplines (and most spiritual disciplines for that matter) focus on the intrapersonal, not the interpersonal.

Even though I do not meditate regularly today, I must acknowledge the authenticity of TM's promise. The sublime high that comes from the discipline of meditating twice daily is quite worth the effort. If Nichiren Shoshu showed me the baby carriage, TM showed me the womb.

What a ride this TM was for me!

"Far out," I said to myself. "I want this walking around!"

That is, until I got greedy and tried to find a way of feeling that cosmic consciousness with my eyes open, not closed in meditation. Then I got sucked into going to the transcendental meditation advanced training, and there I found to my dismay that the guts of this movement was too cult-like for me.

The advanced TM programs were managed by instructors who looked like they had lost their critical thought due to some brainwashing indoctrination.

Yes, I could have just gone back to meditating by myself, but I was disheartened and decided to seek my spiritual highs somewhere else.

Just the same, my ventures into the spiritual marketplace introduced me to a vast underground of people who shared an extraordinary and intimate experience and formed, consequently, a very trusting and powerful bond.
Partly due to my personality, being more of an observer than a joiner, I chose to enjoy occasional spiritual exercises alone.

However, as a result of these spiritual quests, I can now trust and appreciate (and not dismiss as weird or crazy) well-intentioned spiritual movements that attract millions of followers. I am also grateful to have experienced firsthand and deeply understand what hundreds of millions of humans refer to by various names: "The Universe."

There seems to be a drive in humans to feel these altered exotic states, and the elusive emotion called "happiness," which seems to be closely associated. Many of my moments of happiness would result from the mood altering experience described next.

MAGIC MOUNTAIN

While I was open to sampling the spiritual and therapeutic market-place, nothing stuck. I just couldn't relate to any of the gurus and what I found to be their mindless devotees. Nor could I stand the motiva-tional-self-help groups and New Age hype surrounding instant therapy and Western-style enlightenment. I went to my share of "gatherings" to learn about them but was always turned off. Yes, lover of mankind and all, I could no longer spend any more than five seconds with any leader, spokesperson, or member of these cultish outfits.

Then I met Larry Tilley. This was different, and it certainly deserves mention as one of my key formative experiences. Larry was the leader of my first face-to-face communications laboratory and an instructor at the University of Connecticut, where I was attending. Larry ran these human relations groups at his country house in the Berkshire Moun-tains, an inn-like structure surrounded by thousands of acres of farm-land and wilderness: a place that was in appearance and effect, a Shangri-La, the enchanted land depicted in *Lost Horizon*. It also evoked the feel of the healing retreat in Thomas Mann's *The Magic Mountain*, where the combination of isolation from the outside world and the continuous interaction among the patients led to an extraordi-nary level of self-disclosure and emotional intimacy.

I've conducted about seventy-five of these laboratories over the years at Larry's place and another seventy-five at locations throughout the country, making me, I've been told, a candidate for the *Guinness Book of Records*.
Surely, I wanted some additional meaning and direction in my life, but I was so skeptical of the motivation and intellectual competency of any of these groups and movements.

This group dynamic was remarkable. It passed all my tests. And, to this day, it serves to provide the underlying principles and skills of all my work.

Since it affected me so deeply, let me give you, in a sort of diary form, my reaction to my first group session that I had in December, 1972:

I had no idea what to expect. It sounded scary, but I knew I wanted and needed something: Oh sure, I told myself, "I'm OK." Only I wasn't even in tune enough to recognize how lonely I had become. The fields surrounding the Mohawk Trail were deep with snow, and my apprehension grew with the dusk that began to turn the icy-blue blanket to increasingly darker shades of purple…By six p.m. on this dark, chilly December evening, I had reached the little fairy tale mountain village of Charlemont, Massachusetts, where I was greeted by a country inn with an oven filled with freshly baked bread and luscious fish chowder simmering on the stove.

This weekend was one that affected me as none other had before. Until now, I had never had any clearly defined and articulated concept or mission that I could say was mine or say I would live for. That all changed in forty-eight hours.

How different this weekend turned out to be from what I had feared would be some "group therapy" or "rap session." I could present a moment-by-moment description and act out all the players and lines, but it still wouldn't convey the complexity, the brilliance, and the depth of this encounter-group-like experience. I suppose a face-to-face communications laboratory is a slightly different experience for each person who participates in it. For me, it was an event in meeting myself. Everyone in the group was parts of every significant person in my life as well as parts of me!

I saw the scariest of debates and arguments disappear as people in conflict, with the help and support of the group, resolved what seemed to be irreconcilable differences. I saw a process in which the act of getting close enough to someone allows people to sense and probe the feelings beneath the feelings, which are the emotions that are truly motivating the behavior between people. I saw living proof of the words I had so often admired in the work of Hugh Prather in his book *Notes To Myself*, where he reveals: "Once I tell a man I don't like him, I begin to like him." I was watching the corny self-help and spiritual books in action, working, for real, and I knew this was not a cult, not religious or quasi-religious, and certainly not therapy hype. It was the stuff that people try to do but never follow through on.

No gimmicks, no incantations, no gurus, no meditative disciplines, no prayer…just telling the truth.

As the living room's fire burned, as the snow filled the outside fields, I felt every emotion imaginable as I looked at these people who changed from strangers…to friends…to…something more than and different from family.
One member of our group in particular affected me. She was a nun, who would be the first to "get carried away with the pro-cess." She became so touched by the emotional intimacy that she had an irrepressible impulse to face each participant, one by one, and acknowledge some feeling. I watched her move from one to another, slowly coming my way. I hoped she would tire before reaching me. She was OK and all, but how was I to respond to a nun, or anyone for that matter, sitting in front of me gazing into my eyes, giddy from some overpowering moments she seemed to have experienced?

When she encountered me, she sensed my schoolboy-like reaction. I winced as she reached for my hands and looked aside as she searched for my eyes. When I came upon her eyes, the group disappeared. All we did was look at each other in silence. I held her hands and suddenly lost my self-conscious judgments about me, about her and about us. I was enveloped by a long-forgotten sensation: I was delightfully lost somewhere in the world known as the "here and now."

This was the sensation you were supposed to experience. I had entered a disembodied spiritual relationship. Careful! Once you enter this doorway, there is no turning back. Nun, Christian, agnostic, Buddhist,

Jew, atheist, black, white, young, old, male, female…It didn't matter. All those labels disappeared in this encounter process. I was to discover a way to bypass my defensive prejudices and even my own self-criticism.

I found out why I was so afraid of feeling, trusting, getting close; I saw how, why, and when I didn't accept myself and how linked that was to my not accepting others.

What an unfair and controlling parent I'd been to myself!

Emerging from the difficult feelings aroused in me that weekend was a paradoxical joy. I came to understand that I had found myself. That is, after some considerable defensiveness (avoidance, denial, grumbling about this all being phony), I had begun to confess my honest feelings to others in the group. Ultimately, coached to articulate my feelings in a sensitive way, I was able to luxuriate in the exhilaratingly vibrant act of telling the truth, of giving my authentic emotional reactions to what other people said and did. My reactions, right or wrong, shameful or righteous, were out there for others to see.

What a freedom…what a connection…to myself and to others!

As a result of my encounter with this woman and the encounters with all the other group members that followed, I was overwhelmed with a rush, a glow of wonderful feelings. I felt sensations that I seem to recall having had as a child. They were feelings that I wanted so desperately to know again but that were dreadfully out of reach on the path I had been following. I felt the intoxication of trust, of responsible spontaneity, caring authenticity! What an odd and delightful way to be brought back to the wonder of my inner self!

Damn! I knew now that "growing up" did not have to mean growing old and losing the delicious abandon of childhood. I knew that the painful tragedies of mature life, though sobering, would not have to deaden me inside. I knew that being a successful "adult" did not have to mean being buried under a stiff facade of stoicism.

I knew I would someday return again to my "home" inside of me. I learned that making long, sustained contact with my authentic self and connecting with others from that authenticity was "home."

This was my home; my longing stopped; I had found my calling! While these group experiences have had a profound effect on my personal life, the impact on my professional choices has been even greater.

This group process is always with me and provides me with both courage and the necessary techniques, as I enter into what could, I suppose, be characterized as dangerous and unresolvable conflict. I often refer to the face-to-face communications group as "basic training" for organizational development consultants and trainers. Once you've grown comfortable with the level of direct raw authenticity achieved there, and have seen for yourself the scariest of differences aroused and resolved, organizational hijinks, conflicts, and politics seem light.

Now, the trick would be to adapt this utopia to the world of normal interpersonal armor and defenses, without being too out of sync with the rhythm of the "real" world, perceived as a nut, or considered unsophisticated or naive. I knew that this group dynamic was no therapy cult, but how would I convince others, who, just as I had been, would be suspicious?

I had to stay open to what I had experienced and learned and not shrink back to my instinctive defensiveness in the face of real or perceived attack. The world, after all, is not a human relations laboratory, especially not the world of work, and I know as well as or better than most how easy it is to go right back to that old defensive and alienated self after a few interpersonal "disappointments." Help is out there, however, to get us drifters back in line.

How was I to help introduce fellow drifters? How was I to present this quirky-sounding technique to highly resistant clients? How could I adapt this experience to management and organizational development training?

MY LIFE/WORK BALANCE

For twenty-five years, variations of these face-to-face communications laboratories have been a significant part of my work. Even when I'm not conducting a group, I include exercises and experiences in all of my presentations, classes, and workshops that bring about the extraordinary mood and powerful learnings that come only from that unique formula.

Since most of my work involves personal effectiveness and human relations, whether it's called executive coaching, face-to-face communications, presentation training, team building, role negotiation, or leadership, I'm always working at this level of contact.

What a deal! My work is to introduce people to *themselves*; to have them feel and articulate their feelings; to have them let go and feel appreciated and cared for…for *who* they are, not for *what* they've done…and how to do that with and for others.

How many hundreds of times I've seen "the hardest of hearts" melt as they luxuriated in this new world with an added dimension of trust and contact. How many hundreds of times I've shared a knowing nod with that "no-nonsense, strictly-business, street-smart cynic," now fascinated with the experience, who had steadfastly refused to see the leadership potential or the ultimate personal power involved in this form of authenticity. How many hundreds of times I've run a demonstration for a class or group or a team and have had the most resistant of participants ultimately say, "Me next!"

For an educator and counselor, this is a peak experience. (I'm saddened by how few people see their work as meaningful or rewarding; how few are afforded the gratification of such peaks. And I know that the difference most of the time lies in the quality of their business relationships.)

My life/work balance has come partly as a result of having participated in several life/work planning seminars—which has led to my very carefully constructed balance of meaningful work and free time. But my life/work balance is also a function of my dedication to the principles and skills I've learned from the face-to-face communication laboratories. This has provided me with a feeling of aliveness at work, as I have very little tolerance for untrusting relationships with those with whom I work closely.

While I have many of the same disappointments, despairing moments, betrayals, and sorrows as everyone else, I have the tools to adjust my life and change my situations.

These, then, have been the eight most significant events of my life that have shaped my unique fascination with interpersonal and organizational trust.

I, like you, have been shaped not only by my most memorable and peak experiences (high and low), but also by a variety of common experiences related to our shared political, institutional, and cultural history. How these factors have led to a serious but reversible decline in our collective trust is the subject of the next chapter.

2

A THREE-GENERATION JOURNEY

With the end of World War II in 1945, American soldiers returned home to join their families and to become part of a workforce that would contribute to the greatest economic expansion in history. Comparing that time with today, we can also recognize enormous changes in our lifestyle, in the shape and texture of our lives. I'd like to examine some of these changes and focus on how they've affected our sense of trust. What I see over the course of almost sixty years is a progressive decline in trust in our society as a whole, in the institutions that we interact with, and in the workplace. Let's look at how this happened by highlighting the leading indicators of popular culture and the changing political, social and organizational climates over three generations, from 1945 to 1960, from 1960 to 1980, and from 1980 to 2000.

FIRST GENERATION: 1945–1960

Main Street, USA, 1945

Picture a black-and-white newsreel portraying life in the late 'forties. A boy is riding his bicycle, waving to a friendly postman, a playful dog running alongside the bike. His tour takes him down a street of well-manicured lawns and small but cozy-looking homes. A woman is closing the door of her shiny dove-gray Buick with her hip, arms loaded with bags of groceries, smiling a warm "hi" to the boy. A few edits to the sky show the sun, a church steeple, and the moving spokes of the bicycle, leading us to a bustling small town: a barber shop with one chair occupied and three older men sitting in the waiting area, all engaged in a lively conversation; next, a bank window with a dapper-dressed, pencil-mustached president softening an otherwise ominous appearance with a wave of hello; perhaps a bus station with a family dressed in its Sunday best, sitting in the shade of the building's overhanging roof; finally, the soda shop. The bike is carelessly laid down in front of the shop; the boy walks in and is greeted by a bunch of happy crew cuts and pigtails cooing over his new Hopalong Cassidy saddle ring.

The Social and Political Scene

Coming out of the bloodshed of World II and barbarism equal in cruelty to that of any other time and place in history, America in the 'forties and 'fifties experienced a deep need to heal from the recent history of man's inhumanity to man and to return to a social order of peace and community. Families reunited within a culture that, though devastated by personal losses, emerged as a world leader, militarily and financially, physically untouched by the war and with a strong sense of cultural rectitude: America's military and industrial strength had defeated the evils of Nazism and the Japanese Empire.

We also emerged with a renewed faith in democracy, in the brother-hood of all people, and in our society as a successful "melting-pot," blighted though these ideals still were by racial discrimination and seg-regation. A booming economy, domestic political stability, and demo-graphic homogeneity created a sense of comfort and contentment. In spite of fears and tensions that followed the building of the Berlin Wall in 1948, the Russian detonation of an atomic bomb in 1949 and a hydrogen bomb in 1952, and the growing development of the Cold War, most Americans felt safe and secure.

In fact, the international tensions that accompanied the growing Cold War between the U.S. and the Soviet Union strengthened our mood of harmony at home. With Communism as a clearly identified enemy, Americans felt motivated to show that our system of freedom, democ-racy, equal opportunity, and entrepreneurial incentive was superior to a state-controlled and regulated system of government. The 'fifties were the Eisenhower years, a time that identified itself with "peace and prosperity," a time free of the social, ethnic, economic, health, or envi-ronmental crises that we've gotten accustomed to since.

The closest the country came to a domestic crisis in the 'fifties was the McCarthy era of 1951–54, when Senator Joseph R. McCarthy created a political scandal by accusing Communists of infiltrating the highest levels of our government. But after McCarthy was discredited (his most notorious trick was reading the names of so-called "Communist agents" from a laundry list he had), calm returned to political life.
Two advertisements of the period underline this mood of harmony, community and security that postwar America felt. One appeared in magazines in the late 'forties for the new product, television. It showed two adult couples sitting comfortably and chatting while looking at a ten-inch console TV. The idea behind this ad, that watching television is a social or communal experience, certainly doesn't reflect the reality that we've since discovered about TV, namely that it isolates people more often than it brings them together. Instead, the ad reflects the

common belief of the time in old-fashioned togetherness and a rather innocent faith that the impact of new technology would leave these comforting patterns of life intact.

The second ad, which appeared on television in the late 'fifties, was an appeal for racial harmony in America. It showed a cartoon of baseball players of different ethnicities refusing to throw a baseball to or catch it from each other. "Who would want this diamond team? They're diamonds in the rough. A baseball team needs nine good men; one man's just not enough." It concluded by urging viewers not to be like these players: "Americans, join your teammates all. Roll up a winning score." This message for racial tolerance and for America working as a team captures the feeling of community that most Americans had throughout the 'fifties.

In some ways, the first half of the 'sixties continued the political trends of the 'fifties. The Kennedy presidency may have had a more youthful and "with it" style than the Eisenhower presidency, but in substance it was much the same. In spite of his forward-looking image, Kennedy had helped get himself elected by appealing to a military machismo model of leadership when he accused the Eisenhower administration of having allowed a "missile gap" in the arms race with the Soviet Union. His political agenda was basically traditional and conservative: strong defense (including an increased military presence in Vietnam), a military attempt to overthrow the Castro government in Cuba; moderate efforts to deal with the issue of racial segregation; and ongoing efforts to gain the support of conservative Southern Democrats (Kennedy was assassinated on a trip to Texas to mend fences with conservative Democratic Governor John Connolly). At the same time, President Kennedy conveyed a powerful image of charismatic leadership—assertive, intelligent, energetic, and attractive—that reflected Americans' faith and comfort with themselves and their heroes.

True, a new sense of insecurity was in the air. The 1962 Cuban missile crisis brought the U.S. and Russia dangerously close to World War III, and two years later the movie *Fail Safe* (1964), ending with an American president forced to drop a hydrogen bomb on New York City to avoid all-out nuclear war with Russia, showed the terrible dangers of nuclear confrontation. The assassination of President Kennedy in 1963 was, of course, a deep shock to the country, and a prelude to other shocks that were to come. But the economic prosperity of the 'fifties continued without any real hitches into the 'sixties. And while the government was probably more liberal in the early 'sixties than in the 'fifties (actually, Congress had been controlled by the Democrats since 1956), social and political change seemed smooth and gradual.

Looking back on this period, the passage of the Civil Rights Act in 1964 can be seen as consolidating the democratic values of fairness and equal opportunity that Americans have traditionally believed in. By 1965, the Soviet Union and Communist China had replaced Nazi Germany and the Japanese Empire as the enemies of American traditions, but these traditions still seemed secure at home.

Cultural Signposts

To anyone listening to the radio, probably the most influential form of popular literature at the time, the 'forties was indeed a time of peace and trust. Programs like *The Henry Aldrich Show*, *The Fred Allen Show*, and *The Great Guildersleeve* presented a world of small town warmth and friendliness, inhabited by characters that listeners came to know and love, not least because of their quirks and oddities. Even when the darker side of life was recognized in soap operas like *Helen Trent* or crime dramas like *G-Men*, the strong hero or comforting heroine was there to set things right in the end.

When television began to replace radio as a source of drama, comedy and adventure in the 'fifties, programs like *The Jack Benny Program* (with endearing characters like Rochester, Dennis Day, and Mr. Kitzel), *The Lone Ranger*, and *Superman*, (whose hero fought for "truth, justice, and the American way"), continued to reaffirm the values of comfort and trust. Popular shows like *Leave It to Beaver*, *Father Knows Best*, and *The Ozzie and Harriet* Show portrayed peaceful homes, whose most serious dilemmas centered only on the typical pains of childhood and adolescence. *Have Gun Will Travel* and *Gunsmoke* were two popular westerns, typical of a new genre, referred to in those days as "adult westerns," whose stars were understated, but unswervingly dedicated to 'fifties-style moral righteousness, with ethical dilemmas textured in black and white. The marvelously crafted live productions of *Playhouse 90*, with brilliant contributors like Paddy Chayevsky, brought a level of artistic quality to TV, nonetheless capturing a cross-section of viewers, with themes that maintained an underlying faith in human goodness, seeing the world, still, as an overall benign place, free of the more complex problems of later decades.

Pre-baby boomers grew up with heroes and role models like Bob Hope and Bing Crosby, Humphrey Bogart, Bette Davis, Judy Garland, Gary Cooper, Fred Astaire and Ginger Rogers, James Stewart, and Cary Grant. They laughed at the good-natured antics of Laurel and Hardy and The Three Stooges, and at the wit of Jack Benny, Burt Lahr, and Ed Wynn. Whatever real-life moral problems these characters may have had, the public knew little about; scandalous innuendo was modest by contemporary standards.

Disturbing ideas that did arise to challenge this picture of life were channeled into cultural outlets like the science fiction-horror movie, filled with Communist plot paranoia, and with pods, saucers, zombies, and other assorted aliens invading the USA. Our popular culture reflected a confident social consciousness, but one that didn't go beyond the American borders or a rather innocent exploration of right and wrong. Americans by and large were still protecting the two-hundred-year-old ideal of an American Dream utopia, isolated and protected from contamination by other countries, cultures, and values.

Even more serious fictional creations, like William Saroyan's characters enacting the quiet music of the human comedy, John Steinbeck's brooding figures, Ernest Hemingway's wounded heroes in search of direction, or Tennessee Williams's starstruck heroines expressed internal, private, small-group relationships that focused on moral and identity crises, but not on broader cultural/social dilemmas. While a few movies of the 'fifties, like *The Man in the Gray Flannel Suit* and *Invasion of the Body Snatchers* (1956), offered deeper commentaries on the threat and danger of social conformity, most stayed away from this kind of social content.

Westerns continued to celebrate the rugged individualism of the cowboy. Fluffy Rock Hudson-Doris Day comedy romances teased their audiences with hints of illicit sex, only to reassure them at the end that "Love and marriage/Go together like a horse and carriage." New, younger stars like James Dean and Marlon Brando projected a more challenging image of brooding male rebellion and sexuality, but this rebellion wasn't defined in larger social terms. In *Rebel without a Cause* (1955), for instance, it was made clear that if only James Dean's emasculated father would assume his traditional role, take off his apron and be a real man and father, there would be no cause for his son's rebellion.

As for popular music, the lyrics of 'forties and 'fifties ballads and groups were as innocent and free of erotic or violent content as at any time in the history of American music. Crooners like Frank Sinatra and Tony Bennett clothed the erotic fantasies of female audiences in the paternal features of the company bosses their fathers worked for. The advent of Rock and Roll in the early 'fifties and especially of Elvis Presley around 1955 certainly marked a more brazen sexuality and foreshadowed what was to come, but the lyrics remained childlike and innocent. Titles like *The Great Pretender, Teenager in Love,* and *All I Have to Do Is Dream* suggest the soft, dreamy, often self-pitying mood of so many of these songs, quite different from the more confrontational and sexually explicit lyrics of later music. Even into the 'sixties, groups like The Four Tops, and The Four Seasons kept their lyrics innocent and free of social or political themes.

This all changed with the invasion of British Rock, the rise in popularity of folk music with a social agenda, and the entrance of African-American music into mainstream rock, but that's a later story.

The Organizational Climate

Meanwhile, back at the corporate world, American industry was white, male, and paternalistic. Rosie the Riveter returned home to bake and to care for her 2.2 kids, while dad took orders from some boss who had very likely been a military officer. In the decade after World War II, organizations were consciously structured like the military. Lines of command and communication, and conformity to rules were unquestioned. As long as they followed these organizational norms, employees had lifetime job security from a source they trusted as they would a brother or a platoon buddy.

This post-war generation grew up with certain expectations about life and work. Cautious and frugal, parents believed in the value of hard work, and expected that their hard work and loyalty would be noticed and rewarded by a relatively benevolent organization, which would provide them, in exchange, with promotions, opportunities for feelings of belonging, and lifelong job security. To a large extent, until the 'eighties, this promise was kept. If you kept your nose clean, followed the rules, defended and hid behind your boss for protection, and came to work on time, you'd get the security, pension, and gold watch that you were working for. In business and at home, life was predictable and relatively peaceful.

Management training took the form of understanding and reinforcing the rule books while, at the same time, reflective of the moral innocence of the time, management was also willing to examine the effect of human relations training. The T-group (described earlier in its variation, "face-to-face communications laboratories") was inaugurated in 1947 by its founder, Kurt Lewin and a group of colleagues from MIT and quickly became a popular leadership-training tool. Within a few years, thousands of people were to become involved in this training, and its approach was seen by most corporate officers as an excellent balance to an otherwise too-dominating military model of management.

But the T-group phenomenon was to last only a few years into the next decade. The attitudes that emerged from having attended a T-group were often at odds with the authoritarian leadership culture at the office. Work was still a long way from being a participatory democracy, where worker suggestions, let alone worker *feelings*, were solicited.

SECOND GENERATION: 1960–1980

Main Street, USA, 1970

A newsreel circa 1970 would feature college kids, the dominant American profile of the time. A voice-over is accompanied by rock protest music. Oblique camera angles and dozens of jarring edits are used to simulate visions of altered states. The day would still be sunny, but the mood conveyed in this slice-of-life would be alternately bright and somber, juxtaposing sounds and sights of laughter and playfulness with those of crying and angry shouting at protest rallies. An edit would take the viewer to a campus lawn where longhaired adolescents would be seen from behind, gender indistinguishable, playing Frisbee on a college campus meadow. The campus security guard would be seen with a disinterested expression, inured to the sexually provocative behaviors and thinly disguised puffing at marijuana cigarettes. Another edit would carry us to a march on Washington, where the camera would pan across thousands of hippie-looking youth, adorned with clothes, jewelry, hair, and facial hair designed to look outlandish and freakish, living up to one of the youth culture's self-proclaimed monikers: "freaks." Surrounding this assortment of flower children would be an assortment of "hawks"…those who protested the protesters, appearing as hard hats: construction and other "blue collar" workers, rather clean-cut in contrast.

The Social and Political Scene

Whether we call what happened "The Hippie Movement" or "The Counterculture," beginning in the early or mid 'sixties, American society experienced a radical change in values and attitudes. At various levels—government, community, family, and individual lifestyles—a generation of younger people questioned the kind of life they saw around them and the codes people were living by. They were looking for a new openness and spontaneity in their relationships. They questioned or rejected the traditional work ethic, the nine-to-five job, the stable career path, and the conventional marriage, with all the patterns of behavior that went with these values. Hippies, flower children, were looking for a new authenticity. "Don't trust anyone over thirty," they warned. They would have to find their own way because they no longer trusted their elders.

The mid 'sixties was a time of great dreams and excited energy. Student activists and freedom riders were taking the cause of civil rights into the South, along with guitars, marijuana and experiments in communal living. Beginning at Berkeley College in California, and then on college campuses across the country, students protested the Vietnam War, a stodgy academic curriculum ("Why are your libraries so full of tears?" Allen Ginsberg asked in his poem *America*), and limits on their freedom to experiment socially, spiritually, and sexually. The antiwar marches on Washington in the late 'sixties, culminating in the great Woodstock love-in in the summer of 1969 became rallying points for hippies and activists feeling their way toward a new society.

Stable beliefs and political institutions experienced new pressures after 1960. From 1945 to 1960, we had two presidents; from 1960 to 1980, we had five, with one removed by assassination (John F. Kennedy) and one forced from office by the threat of impeachment (Richard M. Nixon). Violence killed or crippled other key leaders—Robert Kennedy, Martin Luther King, Jr., George Wallace, Malcolm X. These tragic losses certainly affected what happened—and didn't happen—between 1965 and 1980.

At a deeper level, this atmosphere of violence shook our faith in democracy as a political process. The death of charismatic leaders like the Kennedys was an emotional blow that we may never have recovered from. Other violent confrontations revealed the deep wounds of division and distrust: the riots and police violence at the 1968 Democratic Convention in Chicago; the series of riots that swept through Newark, Detroit, and Watts in 1968 after the assassination of Martin Luther King; the shooting at Kent State College of student protesters against the bombings of Cambodia in 1970. We seemed unable to find leaders to step forward and rally behind.

And even if we found them, could we trust them? The lingering doubts about the Kennedy assassination led to a growing cynicism about political leaders and the political system. Conspiracy theories flourished. As the Vietnam War dragged on and opposition to it grew, documents appeared suggesting that political leaders like President Johnson, Robert McNamara and Dean Rusk had lied about it. Presidential candidate Kennedy's "missile gap" (which mysteriously disappeared after he was elected) became President Johnson's "credibility gap." Americans simply didn't believe him. The Watergate scandal revealed that a sitting president had dispatched secret operatives to manipulate the primary elections, go outside the law to intimidate political enemies, and break into political and professional offices to steal files; he had then directed government officials including the Attorney General to cover up these crimes and pay off potential witnesses. What an exposé! With this kind of deception and hypocrisy at the top, was any institution safe or any leader to be trusted?

There was also growing suspicion and conflict within the counterculture, and by 1970 it had come apart (if it had ever really existed) as a unified political movement. Militant groups like SNCC (the Student Nonviolent Coordinating Committee) and the Black Panthers had broken from more moderate organizations like the NAACP. Integration, the rallying cry of the 'fifties, was no longer seen as a desirable goal by many African-Americans. A small radical, primarily white group, the Weathermen, went beyond protest and tried to carry out bombings of government buildings. If Woodstock symbolized the height of the hippie dream, the Altamont rock festival in 1970, in which a participant was murdered by a Hell's Angels member hired as a security enforcer, symbolized its dangers and excesses. When Senator Eugene McCarthy, the political choice of the counterculture, lost the Democratic nomination to Hubert Humphrey and the badly divided

Democrats lost the presidential election to Richard Nixon, the dream of democratically bringing about real political change seemed remote indeed.

In the 'seventies, other events, notably the wind-down of the Vietnam War, two oil embargoes, and the continued arms race, caused a further erosion of self-confidence and trust. When the Vietnam War ended in 1973, and it was clear that the U.S. had suffered its first military defeat in history, Americans felt a sense of frustration. People who felt we were right to fight the war were angry that we had "held back" our military commitment; people who opposed the war were angry that we had ever gotten involved. Fifty-seven thousand American soldiers had died for nothing. The Arab oil embargoes of 1973 and 1978 were disturbing reminders of how dependent we were on oil and how economically vulnerable we could be. This was brought home even more when rising oil prices and the resulting increased cost of oil for transportation and industry triggered an economic "stagflation" that continued through the 'seventies and probably cost Jimmy Carter the presidency in 1980. His fate was firmly sealed when the Iranian government held Americans hostage as we stood by helplessly. Finally, under Leonid Brezhnev, the Soviet Union was aggressively expanding its nuclear arsenals. People wondered, "Are we keeping up enough?" All in all, the decade of the 'seventies ended with the growing feeling of weakness in how we dealt with the rest of the world and increasing anxiety about how secure our society and economy were at home.

Cultural Signposts: The Hippie Explosion and its Aftermath

"Come Senators, Congressmen throughout the land,
And don't criticize what you can't understand...
Your sons and your daughters are beyond your command
'Cause the times they are a-changing."

These 1962 lyrics of Bob Dylan's were a rallying cry for a new generation of young people in high schools and colleges, looking at the world
they were going to be working and living in and wanting to change it.

A small group of writers, singers, and entertainers—James Baldwin,
Jack Kerouac, Lawrence Ferlinghetti, Allen Ginsberg, Pete Seeger,
Lenny Bruce, and others of the 'fifties Beat Generation—had laid the
foundation for a shake-up of the otherwise tranquil cultural map that
had prevailed during the Eisenhower years. The impact of their ideas
was enhanced by the explosion of the paperback book trade in the early
'sixties, as countless teens going to college in unprecedented numbers
stormed the bookshelves. Much of their reading was protest and consciousness-raising literature, by such authors as Herbert Marcuse, Erich
Fromm, Alan Watts, and Eldridge Cleaver. A seemingly spontaneous
generation of movements surfaced, all weary of the political hiberna-
tion of the 'fifties and crying for a recognition of their right and pride
to be women, gays, blacks, Native Americans, Marxists, or anarchists.
Sisterhood is Powerful could be seen on the laps of coeds leaning against
campus oak trees.

These early boomers learned, as did the generation before them, much
about life and relationships from the movies. They grew up with new
models of rebellion against social convention in *The Loneliness of the
Long-Distance Runner* and *Billy Budd* (1962), *Bonnie & Clyde* and *The
Graduate* (1967), and *Midnight Cowboy* (1969); and new models of
sexual freedom in *I Am Curious Yellow* (1967) and *Deep Throat* (1968).
Dr. No (1962) and *Yellow Submarine* (1968) challenged the establishment and took this generation on a tour of personal entitlement.

For one idealistic decade, separated from their elders by a "generation
gap," the hippies tried desperately to break away from a dominant culture whose institutions it felt were all too dehumanizing. In a way this
hippie phenomenon was a looking backward as well as forward in time,
telling the story of a wish for a return to real or imagined days gone by

of innocence, openness, sharing, and freedom. In the boom time of the early 'sixties, with its resulting feeling of boundless abundance, with Dr. Spock's "more love/less punishment" child-rearing practices in vogue, with opposition to the Vietnam War as a cohesive rallying point, a new wave of young people nurtured this hippie phenomenon.

Drugs played a major part in the formation and maintenance of the hippie subculture. The passing of a marijuana joint had some sharing as well as illicit accomplice-bonding components. Some hippies simply benefited from the occasional moments of grand vision and insights that would be shared.

Music reinforced the hippie subculture. The soulful cries of the 'fifties folk and protest songs were absorbed in the early and middle 'sixties by Bob Dylan, whose themes expressed a sense of separateness from the dominant culture. Dylan mocked a culture that could neither see nor embrace the idea that "the times they are a changing," relate to a girl who is "just like a woman," or fathom what it's like to be "stuck out-side of Mobile with the Memphis Blues again." While few enthusiasts could agree about the meaning of Dylan's lyrics, they identified with seeing the world in a radically different way from "straight" culture. They felt, in fact, that they were ridiculed, scorned, and hunted for liv-ing the values of freedom, honesty, and openness that straight culture claimed to idealize.

The Beatles were an easier read than Dylan, and for millions, their music, beliefs and life-style reflected and shaped their involvement in the hippie subculture. *Sgt. Pepper's Lonely Hearts Club Band* (1964), the Beatles' groundbreaking "psychedelic" album, spoke for countless alienated and confused young adults searching desperately for a way of following the ideals that were read to them growing up, but for which there were few if any adult role models. Margaret Mead commented that this moment was the first in history where the child would, indeed, be father to the man and where the models of relationships and family bonds would be designed and tested by children without parental guidance.

The Rolling Stones followed right in the wake of the Beatles. Sexual appeal and social revolution went hand in hand with the Stones. *Street Fighting Man* shouted out that "the time is right for violent revolution." Songs like *Ruby Tuesday* and *She Comes in Colors Everywhere* combined a new erotic intensity with a moving tenderness. Other songs like *Sympathy for the Devil* attacked the hypocrisy of the moral and religious values of the older generation. Even more than the smoother and more mellow Beatles, the Stones, with their raw energy and driving rhythms, embodied the youth culture spirit of rebellion.

Dylan, the Beatles, and the Stones were only the most prominent lights in what became a golden age of popular music in the 'sixties. Among folk singers, new voices of protest joined Pete Seeger: Phil Ochs; Joan Baez; Peter, Paul and Mary; Simon and Garfunkel; Buffie St. Marie; Richie Havens. Songs like *The Universal Soldier* and *The War Is Over* attacked the Vietnam War and, in the spirit of the Aquarian Age, all wars. The words from Simon and Garfunkel's title song to *The Graduate* (1967), "Where have you gone, Joe Dimaggio?/A nation turns its lonely eyes to you," were a reminder that the days of baby boomer heroes like Dimaggio were gone. The Doors, Donovan, Led Zeppelin, Jefferson Airplane and Nirvana were just a few of the creators of a new music that celebrated love and sexuality (and often drugs) with a new openness and intensity.

But eventually the hippies were defeated, partly because of inner conflict and partly because of repression by the dominant culture. The Vietnam War, the assassinations, the generation gap, and the consciousness-raising movements that fueled the budding gender, racial, and ethnic pride separation movements, all led to a breakdown of cohesiveness. A key sign of this breakdown was the inability of the hippie movement to maintain its unique image identity and failure to foster its unique community of trust. Non-hippies began to appear, sporting makeshift beards, beads, and bellbottoms. This was the beginning of the end. When the hippie could no longer be distinguished from the weekender, trust began to erode.

And the deep political, philosophical, and moral schism in the United States between the hippies and "the silent majority" that elected Richard Nixon president in 1968 was too overwhelming for the counterculture to overcome. No longer supported by a cohesive rallying point, invaded and divided, and beset by economic hard times (which, in this society, anyway, will topple financially unproductive entities), the hippie movement ended. Haight-Ashbury turned from guitars and flowers to alcoholic binges and drug overdoses. The starry-eyed flower child gave way to the stray freak with an outrageous beard, but the flat, dull, protective, wary look of everybody else. The props and appearances of the 'sixties were appropriated by Madison Avenue and the ever-expanding media, but the spark and spirit had been lost.

The 'seventies was *Donna Summers*, *The Brady Bunch*, and a return to light and bland. Leisure suits and frugality were in, and the decade's two recessions cast a sobering shadow on the American landscape. Most Americans, the Silent Majority included, seemed politically weary, and outside of some outrage toward the Iranians for holding the seventy-nine hostages, news was cool and scarce.

Some box office film hits tell the story of the shift away from the hope and openness of the hippie phenomenon. *Patton* (1970)—General George Patton was a hero of President Nixon's—celebrates a paranoically authoritarian military leader who looks back with nostalgia on the past. *The Godfather I* (1972) and *The Godfather II* (1974) tell the depressing story of how a crime leader, Michael Corleone, turns increasingly ruthless and murderous as he consolidates his power: a story that gains depth by hints that the history of the Corleone family reflects the history of corporate America from 1900 to the present. *Easy*

Rider (1970) has its hippie heroes, played by Peter Fonda, Dennis Hopper and Jack Nicholson, violently murdered by "hippie-hating" rednecks. Another Jack Nicholson movie, *One Flew Over the Cuckoo's Nest* (1975) shows its hero, who embodies the wild, ecstatic spontaneity of the 'sixties youth movement, outmaneuvered and eventually lobotomized by a sadistic authoritarian nurse. *Apocalypse Now* (1973), *The Deer Hunter* and *Coming Home* (1978) are among the prominent anti-war movies of the 'seventies that dramatize how much the lies and brutality of the Vietnam War drained the spirit and hope of Americans. All of these movies, in one way or another, show a painful and severe retreat from the hopes and ideals of the 'sixties.

Perhaps one other less-known movie, *Wild in the Streets* (1969) is the clearest example of how the principles of the hippie movement were misunderstood or exploited by mainstream culture. *Wild in the Streets* is a fantasy about what happens when young people, led by rock star Max Frost, go "wild in the streets," get the voting age lowered to fifteen, elect Max Frost president, take control of the country and put their elders in detention centers, where they wander around like mindless lunatics because LSD has been put in their drinking water. The movie ends with a ten-year-old looking resentfully at Max Frost and preparing to get rid of him because at age eighteen he's over the hill: like true villains, the sinister, amoral members of youth culture turn on themselves. This very bad, very silly movie gives a clear picture of the fear and hatred with which conservative Hollywood filmmakers viewed the 'sixties youth movement by the end of the decade. Particularly notable is its deep sense of distrust between the generations and its demonization of young people.

The 'seventies set in as a counterrevolution to the 'sixties. Some hippies fled to remote underground-like situations and to this day remain dedicated to them. Others fell back in line to a nine-to-five life style. Others straddled the two worlds, trying to get the best from both, a rather difficult compromise.

The Organizational Climate

The baby boomers had to go back to work. By the mid 'eighties, ex-members of the "youth culture" were climbing well into the managerial levels of American organizations. How ironic, after the dreams of the 'sixties, that this group would have to adjust to a work situation that required more hours, while offering relatively less pay and free time than their parents had enjoyed! America had begun to feel the competition emerging from throughout the world, and got shaken right down to its Calvinistic work-ethic roots. Hard times were to come. Management and organizational development training had to deliver programs related to quality and efficiency. Programs such as TQM (Total Quality Management) and other productivity and quality-training strategies were the rage of the 'eighties. These, coupled with dramatic advances in technology, led to significant increases in worker productivity and corporate profits.

As a result of corporate America's need to keep pace with its more productive and efficient global competitors, an era of downsizing emerged. At the same time, organizations squeezed what they could from the remaining workforce. Middle management all but disappeared, replaced by self-monitoring workteams, longer hours and higher standards for productivity and quality. The face of the American worker was now dour indeed. Trust levels would begin to seriously decline. Team-building efforts would attempt to restore morale but could not really manage the growing disappointment, fear and resentment.

THIRD GENERATION: 1980–2000

Main Street, USA, 2000

Now the newsreel is a computer screen, reflecting a collage of different media: videocassettes, camcorders, DVD's, e-mail, and voicemail messages. The landscape is indoors—office, home, school. All are electronically wired. At home, two nine-year-old boys are absorbed in a video game, testing their reactions against simulated environments and imaginary enemies. Kids are seen alone, attached to various screens. "I feel sorry for kids today," laments a hologram of Spike Lee. "They watch computer screens and don't play outside. We played ring-a-levio, Johnny-on-the-pony and stickball." Older kids are chatting on-line, downloading music or searching out movie listings. At school, computer software enables a biology class to explore the ventricles of the human heart, a history class to study the layout of Harlem in 1850, and an art class to visit the Louvre. At home, mom and/or dad are connected to their virtual offices, stealing occasional glances at their beepers, portable phones, or e-mail signaling devices; or checking CNN for latest stock prices, in order to continually up-date their net worth. Edits show a bedlam of diverse languages and customs. The melting pot has been replaced by a tentative pluralism, with millions of voices demanding their space and their audiences. With so many activities going on concurrently, there is a confusion of messages and images. The world of commercials is ubiquitous: on-line, on cable, at movie theaters, at stadiums and sports arenas. There is a frantic cacophony of electronic stimuli.

The Social and Political Scene

After 1980, Presidents Ronald Reagan (1980–88), George Bush (1988–92), and Bill Clinton (1992–2000) reflected a reaction against governmental activism and an effort to decentralize political power by transferring it from what many saw as an overly large and activist Federal government, to state and local control. President Reagan initiated this trend most emphatically as part of a conservative agenda that included an assertively anti-Soviet foreign policy, buttressed by a buildup of U.S. military strength; and a domestic policy that emphasized reducing welfare and other "social benefits" programs, reducing taxation on businesses and wealthier Americans, and reducing various regulatory restraints on the business community. Perhaps President Reagan's greatest economic success was in dramatically lowering the interest rates that were suffered under President Carter, while businesses expanded and jobs grew. The economic success of the Reagan years strengthened the feeling among most Americans that less government interference was better. "Liberal" became a word of some ridicule. Instead, there flourished a traditional faith in American individualism: the belief that self-help is better for people and for the nation as a whole than government contributions for programs like welfare or "tax-and-spend" ideas like federally funded medical insurance and health coverage, urban aid, or aid to education.

Perhaps the greatest triumph of the conservative politics of Ronald Reagan, however, was on the international front where, between 1980 and 1990, first the Communist countries of Eastern Europe were torn by revolt, then the Berlin Wall, symbol of the Communist regime, was torn down, and finally the system of Communist control and the Soviet Union itself collapsed. The arch-enemy of American political values (and a corrupt and inefficient economic and political system as well) had yielded and left the United States as the world's leading superpower, a position strengthened even more by its decisive military defeat of Iraq in the Persian Gulf War in 1990. It also prepared the way for ten more years of unprecedented growth for American business in the global marketplace.

Entrepreneurship and economic concerns, both their successes and their failures, seem to dominate political issues as we enter the twenty-first century, but so does the issue of trust. President Bush's failure to win a second term was influenced by two problems with trust: the collapse of savings and loan institutions across the country (really a betrayal of the trust of investors) and anger at Mr. Bush's agreement to support a tax raise after he had promised at the Republican national Convention, "Read my lips: there will be no new taxes." And although President Clinton's centrist political position seems different from Reaganist conservatism, it is really the economic success of the Clinton presidency—soaring economic growth, almost no inflation, and the elimination of the national debt—that has distinguished it. Certainly it has featured no bold new social programs or political initiatives. The President's one attempt to develop such a program, a national health insurance plan, was an embarrassing failure that probably discouraged him from trying to initiate any further ambitious political projects.

So as we turn the century, the balance of power in the country, morally and politically, seems to be shifting away from its traditional leaders. The various scandals that have followed President Clinton, culminating in the Monica Lewinsky affair, have severely shaken the nation's confidence in his personal morality and integrity and have made it more difficult for him to assert a strong leadership role. Yet there was little support for the Congressional leaders who tried to impeach the President, and the public's respect for Congress and the integrity and relevance of the national electoral process is probably at an all-time low. The recent increase in bias and racial hate crimes, the shocking weapons violence, and problems in our public school system are just some examples of how the leadership of our country seems unable or unwilling to control or regulate powerful disruptive internal social and political forces.

Cultural Signposts

The 'eighties were the decade of the yuppie, successor to the hippie of the late 'sixties and early 'seventies. The yuppie, the self-absorbed, materialistic, upwardly-mobile young urban professional, turned his back on the hippie's search for openness and ecstatic communion. Peter Fonda and Dennis Hopper of *Easy Rider* gave way to Michael

Douglas and Kathleen Turner of *The War of the Roses* (1989). Not to be confused with ex-hippies turned entrepreneurs like Jerry Rubin, yuppies never experienced the emotional commitments of the hippies. A vulnerable and soul-baring rebel like James Dean is replaced in the 'eighties by the figure of James Fox—smooth and likable, but firmly wedded to the comforts and conventions of upper-middle-class life. Surface and status are everything to the yuppie; his too-easily-won cynicism masks inner despair.

With ever more sophisticated acoustic and recording technology, rock and pop music have exploded and assumed various new forms: alternative, gangsta, heavy metal, techno, hip-hop, ska, to name some. And performers like Bruce Springsteen, Eric Clapton, Elton John, John Denver, and Madonna have left a permanent imprint. But the call-to-action/if-you're-not-part-of-the-solution-you're-part-of-the-problem attitude proclaimed by the artists of the 'sixties and 'seventies—The Beatles, The Stones, Dylan, Led Zeppelin, Jefferson Airplane, Nirvana, Jimmie Hendrix, The Doors, Janice Joplin, The Byrds, The Who—is no longer a defining element. Rock and other kinds of popular music have become a background sound to our lives, not a rallying cry or a drumbeat to lead us in a new direction.

To a large extent, the same combination of bottom-line economics and computer technology that has transformed the business world has also transformed the world of popular culture. The small rural communities out of which jazz, folk music, country music, and old-fashioned rock and roll developed are gone or disappearing. To survive today, filmmakers, writers, musicians, and other artists need financial backing, selling strategies and communications technology to successfully market themselves and their products. To survive, the performer has to keep his or her eye on the bottom line. This entrepreneurial pressure may encourage production, but it also limits artists by forcing them to please a mass, standardized audience. How many films show the "good guy" or "good gal" not winning in the end (after going through all sorts of exaggerated dangers first)? How many films with fast action, fireballs and explosions explore—or even show—the real damage this kind of violence produces? How many films show the real nature of work? The ever-accelerating use of technology and increasingly competitive marketing pressures encourage this kind of "yup-piedom" in the popular arts today.

That said, films during the past twenty years have still addressed real issues of concern in America. *Thelma and Louise* (1991) dealt with social oppression against women; *Philadelphia* (1993) was the first major film to argue for a sympathetic understanding of the AIDS epidemic that cast a fearful shadow over the decade of the 'eighties (it also shows how an amoral yuppie, played by Tom Hanks, is transformed by his tragic illness into a caring, sympathetic figure). *Wall Street* (1987) exposed the ruthless unscrupulousness of the stock scams of the late 'eighties. And a box office star like Tom Cruise—*Top Gun* (1988), *The Firm* (1995), *Jerry McGuire* (1996)—still served as a hero and role model.

But distrust, cynicism, and an increasingly deliberate exploitation of violence also mark films of the past twenty years. In films like *Scarface* (1983), *L.A. Confidential*, *The Rock*, and *Face-Off* (1997), the crime and gangster movie flourishes, often with suggestions of uncertainty about who the criminal is and who the law enforcer is. (*Face-Off*, for instance, features the bizarre plot of a police detective and a criminal both undergoing radical facial surgery—hence the title—to change identities with each other.) Quentin Tarrentino's smash hit, *Pulp Fiction* (1996) offers a seamy world of brutality, drugs, scams, and betrayals, with characters whose dialogues seem totally detached from the violence that they perpetrate. While the subject matter, violent crime, is common enough, Tarrentino's arch, almost smirking style of dialogue and action shows a new cynical sophistication that presents violence as an object of humor. The spate of recent films imitating *Pulp*

Fiction—Get Shorty (1995), *Swingers* (1996), *Grosse Point Blank* (1998) shows the influence and popularity of this technique.

Conspiracy plots loom large in recent films, and they go far beyond the fairly direct assassination conspiracy theory of a film like Oliver Stone's *JFK* (1992). The drug industry conspiracy plot of *The Fugitive* (1995), the police department conspiracy plots of *Mulholland Falls* and *L.A. Confidential* (1997), and the law corporation conspiracy plot of *The Firm* (1995), taken together, portray the nets of deceit, corruption and murder as deeply embedded in the highest and most influential echelons of society.

Another insight into how our sense of trust has eroded over the past generation is provided by comparing two widely-viewed science fiction TV series, *Startrek* from the 'seventies and *The X-Files* from the 'nineties. *Startrek* embodies the liberal, social reformist belief system of the 'sixties as well as the faith in organizational leadership inherited from earlier times. The *Startrek* crew embraces the confidence that American democratic, problem-solving values can transform the world and projects it into outer space, along with the liberal faith that different groups can resolve or accept their conflicts and live together harmoniously. Political and organizational skills supplement and even replace the simplistic military-based models of heroism of an earlier America. The mood and focus of *The X-Files*, on the other hand, is vastly different. To begin with, Mulder and Skully, the heroes, are defensive and xenophobic, not outward-directed: In their adventures, they are defending us and themselves from aliens, or from monstrous or criminal entities threatening to invade our way of life. Even more importantly, The *X-Files* has a totally conspiratorial view of our government and of world leadership in general, portraying the F.B.I., in collaboration with a vague, sinister alien group, as plotting to infiltrate and destroy the human race. The despair, pessimism, and paranoia, as well as the anti-democratic assumptions, of this immensely popular series are a disturbing comment on the cynicism and distrust of organizational leadership that has swept over our society since the 'sixties and 'seventies.

The Organizational Climate

If the organizational structure looked like an hourglass in the mid 'eighties, by the mid 'nineties, it looked, according to Bob Jud, a change management thinker and practitioner, like "a Hershey bar with an almond in the middle of it." The flattened organization is here to stay, it seems. Temporary project teams, not departments, dominate the organizational landscape.

Organizational change, some say, is as lightning-quick as tech-nology change (which used to be every six months, but now it's probably every three). Everyone has to manage his or her own career. Gone are the days when your boss took care of your future and your flanks. Gone are the days when you could put away your resume for a while after you landed a job. Gone are the days when you could keep a low profile and just do your own good work without having to publicize it throughout the organization.

Training programs in the 'nineties have shifted to adapt to the service and information culture that America has become. Clearly, our eco-nomic world hegemony is now due to our having cornered the "intel-lectual" markets, encompassing science, technology, medicine, finance; and software for everything from pocket toys to pace-makers to smart bombs. Computer and software-design skills are high on the list, fol-lowed by personal skills, like executive or personal style and presenta-tion coaching, counseling/persuasive skills, and project and team leadership. Underlying all of these skills is the ability to arouse and facilitate feelings of trust.

It seems everybody is living from quarter to quarter. Lots of move-ment, lots of shuffling, lots of rumors, lots of e-mail and voice-mail.

To whom do you turn? Who will stand up for you against an injustice? No wonder the workforce is turning to lawyers for protection! There is prosperity, an abundance of part-time work (with no benefits), and an abundance of full-time, demanding jobs with long hours. Senior managers, with the help of investment bankers are structuring fantastic deals and golden parachutes for themselves, and the gap between them and the average worker is the widest I've seen in twenty-eight years in the business. We are in the midst of a crisis of trust in many of our American organizations.

Where Are We and What Can We Do?

"Times, they are a-changing" very rapidly! Markets and technology change continuously. The pace is exhausting and exciting, and to keep up with the demands of a global economy, business has to be more efficient than ever. According to most surveys, working Americans over thirty see the past decade as the most stressful in their history. It's probably been the most stressful of the twentieth century, and the stress will continue into the twenty-first. Throughout this book, there are "trust-nets" you can use to reduce this stress and recapture the trust.

How to recapture the trust is what the rest of this book is all about.

3

THE CRUCIBLE OF TRUST

The crucible of trust at work lies in the relationship of supervisors and those whom they supervise. Unless you own a company, lock, stock and barrel, there's someone you report to. And if you've been with an organization for any length of time, there may well be people whom you supervise or, at the least, give direction to. It is important to remember that anyone, at any level in the chain of command, yourself included, can make life heavenly or hellish for the people below.

By this time, you should have a pretty good idea of my thoughts and feelings about trust. Now lets evaluate your tendency to trust or to distrust. And let's assess your sense of how trusting your workplace is in general.

First, let's take a look at your situation. Respond to the questions on page 88 by indicating if the identified actions occur: Never or Rarely (1 point), Sometimes (2 points), Often (3 points), or Almost Always (4 points), as they relate to your experiences with your supervisor/supervision at your present work-place.

1	I can't express contrary opinions or disagreements	⇨ _____
2	I am intimidated or controlled	⇨ _____
3	I am taken advantage of	⇨ _____
4	I suspect hidden agendas	⇨ _____
5	Commitments are not honored	⇨ _____
6	Roles and responsibilities are vague	⇨ _____
7	Misunderstandings build up due to a lack of timely feedback	⇨ _____
8	Highly personal data has not been kept confidential	⇨ _____
9	I withhold my personal vulnerabilities	⇨ _____
10	My supervisor has plagiarized my ideas	⇨ _____
11	Feedback tends to be cutting and unproductive	⇨ _____
12	I can't offer corrective feedback	⇨ _____
13	I am a number, not a valued partner	⇨ _____
14	I have witnessed unethical or unprofessional behavior	⇨ _____
	TOTAL YOUR SCORE	⇨ _____

A score of above twenty-eight points suggests that you are part of a rather untrusting work environment. You must be feeling rather negative and cynical right now.

If you scored between fourteen and twenty-eight, you probably feel quite trusting of your supervisor (or supervisors) and must feel that, with respect to these issues, you have a good situation.

Now, in order to assess your sense of how trusting your workplace is in general, indicate whether the values or norms on page 90 are mostly <u>true</u> or mostly <u>false</u>.

		T	F
1	People can express their opinions	☐	☐
2	People can take risks and try creative strategies	☐	☐
3	Senior management is honest in spirit and behavior with its mission and value statements	☐	☐
4	Working agreements are clear	☐	☐
5	Performance reviews and evaluations are fair	☐	☐
6	Termination procedures are fair	☐	☐
7	Expectations are clear among departments	☐	☐
8	Effective interpersonal skills are valued and rewarded	☐	☐
9	Civility is valued	☐	☐
10	Differences are honored and diversity is seen as beneficial to the organization	☐	☐
11	Teamwork is valued	☐	☐
12	There are competitive and fair compensation and incentive programs	☐	☐
13	Promotions tend to be based on results	☐	☐
14	Management, from the senior level on down, listens to reactions, needs, and feelings from others, regardless of their position or status	☐	☐

The scoring is very simple. If your response to any of the questions was "mostly false," that item is probably a problem and bothers you and a lot of people in your organization. If more than three of your responses were, "mostly false," you probably see your organization as rather untrustworthy and probably have a rather cynical view of life in your organization.

Whatever your overall assessment of these two sets of questions as they apply to your situation, the purpose of this chapter is to help. If your relationship to your supervisor (or supervisors) is less than perfect, you will find comfort in knowing that these situations exist in many places, and things can be and are being done for improvement. Continue reading for additional ideas, "trustnet" tips and inspiration. If your feelings about your supervisory relationships are positive, continue reading for confirmation of the good things that are likely going on around you along with some of the specific things that you can do and reinforce to maintain this healthy environment.

While you may be spared some personal angst by having good supervisory relationships, a low trust organization takes its toll eventually, leading to dysfunctional behavior, negativity, and a spiraling decline of trust throughout the organization. Wherever you are in the organization, you can help to reverse that decline or sustain the good feelings.

Continue reading for suggestions about what leaders and other plain folks can do to nurture "functional" behaviors to generate and recapture the trust and create a more perfect situation.

But before explaining more about regaining trust, it would be helpful to further explore just what trust is. What is this special quality that so many people in personal and organizational relationships feel has been lost?

Trust comes from the German word "Trost," meaning "comfort." There's a deep truth to this simple definition; what a lovely thought it is to be comfortable with someone or some situation.

But what creates and sustains the feeling of comfort associated with trust? In the world of organizations, trust is an amalgam of many factors. Here's a summary of successful behaviors practiced by the professionals and pioneers from my practice whose work and results I know well:

In their book *Credibility*, Norman Posner and David Kousies identify trust as the number-one most critical characteristic of leadership. They use the word "credibility" as it is used in a courtroom when defining an acceptable witness. In order for the testimony to have credibility, the witness must be seen as <u>competent</u> enough to perceive and articulate the situation, and he or she must be believed to have <u>fair intent</u>, by having nothing to gain personally by deception. As you'll see soon, these are both basic elements of what trust involves.

Based on the interviews and research related to this book, I would say that the following seven conditions of trust are essential to supervisory and organizational trust:

- Freedom from fear

- Non-deceptive intentions

- Role clarity

- Risk taking

- Mutuality and sharing

- Task-related competence

- Interpersonal sensitivity

What do these conditions of trust look like in organizations today?

Let's look more closely at these concepts, and in order to derive some good working definitions, at what some mentors and practitioners in the world of organizations have to say about these conditions as they relate to interpersonal relations in the workplace.

FREEDOM FROM FEAR

At work, most people are afraid much of the time, and fear is dysfunctional. Intimidation paralyzes creativity and productivity. Of the many challenging, provocative, and brilliant suggestions promoted by Edward Demming, the management consultant/industrial psychologist credited with having built the post-war Japanese corporate empire, "driving fear out of the workplace" is one of his most central and most often cited.

How many times have you sighed with relief on realizing that you weren't caught being late? I used to meet with a very senior-level executive whose behavior proved that movement up the corporate ladder does not necessarily guarantee freedom. At the end of the day, he would listen for sounds and motion in the next office. He would never leave for home until he was sure that his boss had already left for the day.

"When does that paranoia end?" I've asked many senior officers. "Never" is the choral response. "We have more guns pointing towards our heads than ever." After years of potshots, a norm of harassment ensues.

George Kenney, partner and CIO at the Nicholas Applegate Asset Management firm in San Diego, spoke to me about his shift away from an authoritarian fear-driven management style after his move to southern California: "I've finally been able to integrate the 'soft side' of management into my otherwise results-driven management style, which, as you know, served me so well back East. At my last position, for example, I would say, 'I have no time for incompetence, nor do I have time for the unfortunates.' Not anymore. Not here, anyway. In this competitive field of Information Technology, we have to practice a more humanistic and trust-oriented approach in order to attract and retain talent."

Kenney reminisced about the old days of intimidation, characterized by "a pit-in-the-stomach" feeling...We'd always be on guard for a swipe or a snipe...in an organizational culture characterized by blaming, destructive criticism, and competitive jockeying for position." Does Kenney now feel out of sync with this older, more authoritarian management system? To this question, he remarked, "For some other units and individuals in this and other organizations, this humanistic and collaborative approach may be ill-fitting and dysfunctional, and some people's personality and job requirements may be better suited to control and stress. But, in my service end of the business, people tend to thrive on respect and tranquility."

Mark Mula, Director, Leadership and Management Development, for Warburg Dillon Reed Swiss Bank, asserts that "Organizations are becoming more and more 'short-term' stays." Many of us remember lifetime employment, but today's norm is more temporary relationships. With short stays in organizations, how does trust develop? Up through the mid 'eighties, people were allowed some six to nine months to adapt to a new organization. Today, new employees are expected to "hit the ground running." Employers expect people to get a feel for the job and culture and start making contributions and taking risks right away. To get this rapid a level of openness to the point of asserting one's views about the business, new employees have to feel a high level of respect and acceptance. In addition to choosing rather open and assertive individuals to begin with, organizations have to involve employees in team situations bolstered by the kinds of face-to-face communications training outlined in Chapter Five. There is no other way I know of to generate the rapid trust that enables employees to "hit the ground running."

One personal experience of mine illustrates the negative impact of low-trusting organizational norms. While I like to think of myself as rather assertive in group settings, certain group norms can intimidate me into silence. I was a junior staff member in one organization, where I saw that anything said by any junior person elicited a murmur of snide remarks. Some aspect of any assertion, however justified or well-intentioned, would be seen as foolish by some strategically placed person whose job, it seemed, was to make a crippling, acerbic remark to generate a flash reaction. Damn if I was going to say anything in that group! I chose the role of a shy, low-presence member over that of an idiot. On two occasions, however, I couldn't avoid having to make some public response. My anxiety was so high that I ended up uttering some gibberish that embarrassed me even more. While I heard nothing in my presence, I'm sure the chorus rang, "No wonder he never says a thing."

While "surviving" emotionally is supremely important to us all, let's not forget surviving financially. Since the early 'eighties, few organizations have been able to promise lifetime employment. Even the concept of a working contract with a predetermined promise of notification, and severance is rare. No, most of us work under some variation of "termination at will."

Kadri Ajileye is Assistant Director of Medical Service at Central Bank, Lagos, Nigeria. "When I lived in Nigeria, trust, as you define it, didn't exist. All decisions were political. The Hausa tribe was in power, and if you were of the Yoruba tribe, you were discounted. As a member of the Yoruba tribe, I knew what it was like to have no 'security.' I know the difference between living under someone's whim or mood, and living under an agreed document that contains very direct and timely feedback and reviews."

Probably the most controversial issue that has arisen from all of my interviews and discussions is that of honesty about dismissal and quitting. Of course, both parties are at risk: inform people months before you fire them, and they'll either quit or start looking and slack off; tell your employer that you're looking, and you may suffer any number of indignities, which might well include immediate dismissal.

Overall, there seems to be an acceptable norm of implied reciprocity around this particular dilemma: "I don't expect you to tell me about your plans to terminate until a certain agreed or implied amount of notice." The amount of time varies related to such factors as position, level, and time to find a replacement. The critical factor in maintaining trust, however, is always the degree to which the employer lets employees know where they stand through clear standards and performance reviews so they can "see it coming" if they are at all awake. (It's interesting to note that the same kind of pre-warning to the employer prior to quitting has never been brought up in any of my conversations.)

Keith Mullin, CEO of Mullin and Associates/Lincolnshire, an outplacement and executive coaching consulting firm in New York City, adds: "Once you inform your employees of your intent to dismiss them, let them go right away; don't let them linger around as dead wood and decay amidst a thriving group to which they once belonged. The most humane thing to do is to let them go as soon as possible with as much help as you can afford. A combination of a fair severance along with professional outplacement guidance goes a long way in promoting trust inside and outside of the organization."

In numbers-driven organizations, it's often difficult to admit to a mistake. A lapse of memory, a "senior moment," a misplaced file, or absent data, all can lead to serious admonitions. Elaine Franklin, Manager of Public Affairs and Corporate Communications at Pepsico, Inc. in Purchase, New York, has the unique pleasure of working in such a pressure environment without the dread of making a mistake. "It's so calming and enlivening to be with a chairman who is free to admit to his own imperfections. It frees the rest of us from having to pretend that we know it all and feeling that we must cover up the slightest mistake. The people who realize this are far more productive, welcoming challenge and feedback and making corrections that make their work even better."

NON-DECEPTIVE INTENTIONS

Most people at work are wary of being deceived. People tend to remember promises, however casually they may have been offered. If you are a parent, you have undoubtedly often heard your child insist, over your protest, that you promised something to him or her. While you may deny such a promise, if you are really honest, you may remember a moment when…well…you did say something about a toy or candy as a reward.

I believe initial promises are rarely forgotten and—if kept—create strong emotional threads of attraction and retention. Sloppiness about promises and expectations is one of the greatest problems in American business today. I know that the biggest reason why I and many others like me may "resist change" is our sense that the promises used to lure us to new positions or activities will be breached. I once left one job for another only when assured that I would have identical freedom to make my own schedule (a situation I cherished at the time). Circumstances changed at the new location, and my freedom to manage my own schedule was compromised. Although I understood the business needs that created this change and accepted the requirement, I resented this breach of promise and dragged my feet as I inched towards a lethargic compliance.

And be careful! People tend to collect on broken promises. Employees of a retail client of mine told me of the clever way in which some employee stole in clothing, the equivalent of a broken promise of a bonus that never came. In this situation, the store-owner's greedy and deceptive behavior led to such resentment that the employee was determined to do whatever was felt necessary to even the score.

Document your promises. For any number of reasons, we all have selective memory. Write out all interpersonal contracts. This written documentation can act to implement deserved rewards while reducing the perception of deception.

Social psychologists show pictures and videos of people exhibiting various expressions, as well as verbal and non-verbal behaviors, and then ask people for their reactions to what they saw. As you might guess, the variety of interpretations is as wide as the variety of personalities viewing the situations. The lesson: People often ascribe motivations to what you say or do, so whenever possible, you'd better be really clear about your reasons for your actions that may affect another. You can't over-communicate your intentions.

Marianne Gaige, CEO of Cathedral Corporation, a high-tech electronic imaging Company headquartered in Chatham, New York, sums up her view of recapturing the trust in one word: kindness. "I want my managers to have and utilize power with authority and kindness. This means that unpopular decisions are made and executed without ever having to take advantage of anyone. It means keeping promises. Trust is telling the truth. Telling the truth is essential. How deadly it is to promise something to someone that you either know you cannot deliver or don't really have the information or authority to deliver. A reckless promise based on some partially formed wish and desire to keep a person motivated is destructive to trust. There is also that fine line between being truthful with someone (as you see it) and being meddlesome or micro-managing that person. I can't tell you how difficult it is for me sometimes to 'bite my tongue' and let someone do it his or her way. Often I learn useful alternatives that way."

We trust those who make us believe that they are telling the truth and that they have nothing to hide. All of us have seen, however, that withholding and manipulation is the norm at many organizations and that deception, and the suspicion of deception (which leads to unfortunate but common mutual duplicity), are all too frequent.

Sherry Harris, former Senior Vice President of Education and Human Resources at Clinique Laboratories, and currently Head of Human Resources at Wards, insists, "A clear sense of the organization's direction and mission, along with policies and strategies that support those values, define organizational trust."

Scott Darrah, Human Resource Manager at IBM, has observed lots of "culture change" at his company. No organization is better known than his for the shock of downsizing and the potentially deleterious effects it may have on employee morale and trust. "The single most important lesson for IBM and all the other organizations who have had to downsize is <u>overcommunicate</u>. Give straight talk from the beginning. Communicate more than you think is necessary."

A lot of people are suspicious of senior management's integrity, sometimes with good reason, at other times unfairly. And despite a climate of suspicion on the part of management as well as employees, trust can be recaptured by the consistent fit between word and deed.

So as not become too myopically dismayed with our own organizational landscape, consider the optimism of Irina Filipova, Developmental Officer at the International Peace Academy (IPA), the conflict mediation unit of the United Nations. In Irina's world, trust and breaches of trust have life and death implications. When we spoke in 1996, she commented that both the quality and quantity of world use of their services was at an all-time high. Despite the fact that some thirty-four wars were being waged in twenty-nine locations between 1993 and 1995, countries were contacting the IPA in record numbers to settle and/or avert national and international disputes.

In 1998, Irina's response was still upbeat, although it sounded a bit more sober: "The issues that lead to national and international war and peace are much too complex to be understood in terms of 'trust.'" she said, recognizing that in international pol-itics deceptive behavior is expected and perhaps even encouraged: "Remember, in realpolitik terms, it's in the best self-interest of all political leaders not to trust. As a result of the end of the Cold War and the end of the superpowers managing their interests in various parts of the world, more violent sub-regional conflicts have come about. There have been a lot of failures, I know. Look at the recent history of peacekeeping efforts at the U.N." Nevertheless, Irina knows that she and her organization's mission of mediation are part of a process that antedates Solomon. Her gratification must be in knowing that these services yield small, sometimes imperceptible, rewards, appreciated sometimes, scorned sometimes, viewed indifferently the rest of the time.

Honesty and directness are also a valuable part of an organization's public policy. Any organization should have a clear mission and vision statement. While this bromide has been around for a long time, so has employee cynicism about it. Mission and vision statements generally say wonderful things about such promises as "corporate integrity," "hard work," "worker and customer dedication," or "devotion to quality and excellence." But, as Sherry Harris points out, "Companies have to announce a greater purpose beyond rivalry-oriented goal-setting, beyond motivational hype, and beyond hollow mission statements that few employees believe to be honest. Corporations have lost so much time," she laments. "All we have to do is align the company's values with those of its people. Let them state what their values are. Let them state what their mission and visions are. Beneath our noses is the formula for recapturing the trust!"

ROLE CLARITY

Trust increases when we share our expectations with another and when that other responds positively to those needs. Most people are incapable of reading others' minds. Too often we assume people know what our requirements are. Indeed, they rarely do. We have to communicate our needs and expectations clearly. So often, trust is broken due to a perceived breach of a perceived promise. How doubly sad, yet how common this situation is. How often we misinterpret someone's intention on the basis of an incorrect assumption about someone else's responsibility! Remember the dictum about the word "assume:" It makes an *ass* out of u and *me*.

When I was a senior in high school, I worked as a cashier at a supermarket. After about a week, my responsibilities were increased to those of a clerk, a job I didn't want. After a day of denting cans that I dumped off a conveyor belt and taking four hours (instead of the normal one) to fill the vegetable trays with ice, I was called to the office. I protested that I signed up as a cashier, and this backbreaking labor wasn't my job. The manager then made me re-read my employment agreement, which included the word "clerk" somewhere in the fine print. This was to include, besides stacking cans and bags of ice, a variety of other onerous jobs such as gathering shopping carts from the parking lot in the rain, loading garbage dumpsters, and maintaining the bathrooms. Being a passive-aggressive teenager, I completed these tasks with a combination of such sloth and incompetence, that I was soon back behind the cash register as a permanent cashier.

With all working contracts, take the time necessary to ensure that all parties read all the print—fine and large. Revisit the understanding from time to time, especially those conditions you know to arouse confusion and misinterpretation.

Scott Darrah discovered from his eighteen years at IBM and his Master's Thesis research on the effects of downsizing that "the supervisory relationship is the essential ingredient in organizational trust." However distant and maligned senior management may have become (fairly or unfairly), along the company grapevine, trust and confidence in one's immediate supervisor far outweighs the divisive rumor mill.

One way to keep that trust is to periodically review one another's needs, expectations, and role description, adjusting them as necessary.

The importance of having a clear sense of another's position cannot be overemphasized. Trust flourishes when personal and interpersonal barriers are diminished. In politically charged organizations, people tend to hide behind ambiguous roles and vaguely worded or never-worded responsibilities. Clarifying relationships between workers, within groups, and between groups takes time and courage.

Marianne Gaige has developed some strong feelings with respect to role clarity. So much of the work she has had to do to empower the managers and the work force at her plants has started with the acknowledgment of position, role and responsibility. "When roles and responsibilities are ambiguous," she asserts, "there is no leadership! There are so many decisions that can be made, but they are not: people feel helpless, and inevitably an inappropriate party will fill that power vacuum. No question, the first step in organizational renewal and recapturing the trust is to have roles clarified, negotiated, and set by the people in those roles."

Jane Maloney is an organizational development consultant reared on a combination of organizational development technology and psychodynamic interpretations of organizational behavior. Expertly aware of the multiple personal and interpersonal factors that will affect collaboration, she starts with role clarification and the charting of standards and responsibilities. "Once you have agreement on your role and the role of others with whom you are working, then the personal and group dynamic trust issues and dilemmas can be seen more clearly for what they are. Sometimes I find that those interpersonal issues are solved by the role clarification itself."

Maloney's responsibility charting is one effective method of role clarification. Responsibility charting is a technique that involves all parties in identifying significant business activities and agreeing on what role each player has in the life cycle of each activity. Purchasing an expensive piece of equipment might be such an activity. The joint responsibility charting procedure might give someone from senior management the role of being informed and ultimately responsible for authorization. Someone in middle management, say a department head, may need to be "cc'd." The supervisor overseeing the operation of this equipment may be the one who articulates the need, examines allocations, and specifies the equipment; and someone in accounting may simply cut the check. For these and other seemingly simple operations, lines of responsibility are often not well thought out and necessary items get sandbagged by people who think they should have been consulted.

Leaving responsibilities to day-to-day whim is not empowerment. Freedom can be chaos. Even for the more professionally skilled, work structures and some orchestration are needed to create a lively, empowered organizational environment capable of mindful and rational improvisation. There need to be some basic parameters, ground rules, and agreements. As with a jazz improvisational group that agrees on musical structure, key, and basic melody, team members agree on basic structure, reporting mechanisms and staple responsibilities for optimal freedom and collaboration.

Ben Weisman is a former dean of the Long Island University Graduate School of Business. With a Ph.D. in finance and a specialty in venture capital; and with experience as the go-between on literally scores of deals at the IPO level of complexity, he has some strong thoughts on the importance of trust among dealmakers. Ben explains, "There isn't the typical concept of trust at work in the world of venture capitalists. Their own personalities and the nature of the business call for some level of deception in order to get the most out of a deal. However, all conscious parties are aware of this reality. On a personal level, I know this type to have great hearts, and they will lend or give away their precious money in a heartbeat. But, be open and self-disclosive to a competitor during a deal? Absurd!"

Weisman takes a skeptic's view of truth and trust in the corporate world, but not a despairing one. When asked how he feels about the backstabbing competition common in American corporations, his advice is, "Don't turn your back. The point," he argues, "is that in the venture capitalist's world, the deception and nastiness is more often up front…you know it and they know it. It's part of the game and people have to go to where the rules fit their temperament and needs. Some couldn't live without a war-like stress.

"Every person has different rules of what is right and what is wrong when negotiating. It is vital to know what a person's 'house rules' are. Contracts in writing can clarify what each person regards as 'the deal.' A handshake among peer players may be enough. But if the others do not consider you a 'player,' they can and usually do try to pay you nothing. A new player would be like a neophyte sitting down at a poker game with an experienced group of sharks. Ask what the rules are; many people will tell you, but some won't."

Julie Casella, an eighteen-year veteran of Chase Manhattan Bank, emphasizes how measurable standards and expectations support role clarity in organizations. She has successfully ridden through three mergers and is now a Vice President of Human Resources, servicing some very powerful units of the bank. Very much involved in performance management, she respects the integrity of her bank's program of performance and evaluation. "For us at Chase, trust is a function of performance and reward, and we put the two together in a concept called 'performance culture.' Performance culture is a compilation of behaviors including mentoring, feedback, measurable standards, straightforward communications, and support instruments. This has everything to do with trust because it demonstrates trust: the clarification of expectations and the rewards when expectations are met. Conversely, when expectations are not met, trust is maintained by having clear, standard, and fair ways of 'managing someone out.'"

RISK TAKING

All trust implies that a certain amount of risk and vulnerability exists between individuals. The word "trust" implies an equality between people that limits the fear of vulnerability: I trust you not to make me regret my openness with you. In most of our everyday interactions, even among intimates, however, this level of trust is rare. Most organizational climates encourage their members to "play it safe," that is, to avoid unconventional or risk-incurring behavior that might expose them to harm.

In organizations, harm usually comes from some form of punishment related to unwanted behavior. In some cases the definition of "unwanted behavior" in organizations is drawn so broadly that creative and innovative thinking is actively discouraged.

"Can I trust you?" A colleague at a company I once worked for asked me. "What do you mean?" I asked. "Well, I'm so paranoid that whatever I say will get back to management," she said. "I'm sure at least one person is a spy, and I'm afraid I can't say anything to anyone without it going back." Well, I knew I wasn't a spy, and I knew what she was talking about because I had long ago decided to watch everything I said at this place. But suddenly I began to worry that she might be setting me up. I remembered that classic line from the 'fifties version of *Invasion of the Body Snatchers*: "Sure I love you, Bill, but how do I know you're not one of them?" After a brief checking-out period, we both took the risk and revealed our mutual disregard for the one we both suspected was the biggest rat anyway. Surrounded by rats for colleagues and skunks at the helm, neither of us was meant for a long tenure at this zoo. While I know that the owners were "crying all the way to the bank," I also know how much more they could have been making and how much less grief they could have sustained.

Provoke risk taking by taking risks yourself. Ask for feedback about specific actions you have taken. Prove to your people that there will be no danger in this. Build a team where the word is: "What a luxury; there's no BS—you can say almost anything to anybody here."

Yet paradoxically, being willing to remain open to risk helps build trust and confidence. You know you're in a trusting situation when you feel comfortable and at ease. You feel secure and accepted for who you are, and you don't feel that you have to prove yourself over and over again.

Monroe Millstein, President and owner of the international chain of clothing stores, Burlington Coat Factory, has always wanted to be seen as a trusted "uncle" to all of his employees. "If you have a problem," he announced, in a videotape that was played to the employees in each of his stores, "you call me personally and I'll respond to you personally!" (How different from the detached images that many business owners tend to communicate!) With many of his actual family members working alongside of him, Monroe has always wished to convey a feeling of family and home to his employees. He sees comfort as a major component of worker satisfaction and trust.

In order to free employees to be their creative best, supervisors must show patience, understanding and respect. Blame and criticism erode, while flexibility and acceptance enhance, trust and productivity.

For trust to flourish, it helps to have an organizational culture that permits some error. I've worked at places where I felt that if I confessed an error, I'd be out, regardless of my past record. I know of a half-dozen organizations whose employees say, "You're never more than thirty seconds away from being fired here."

Michael Boyle directs the Creative Services Division at Foote Cone Belding/Leber Katz Partners, one of the largest *Madison Avenue*-type ad agencies. (Ad agencies remind me of human ant colonies. Their hallways are teeming with energy and motion.) In response to a question related to one of my favorite mottoes, "Ask forgiveness, not permission," Boyle cautions, "It depends on how creative and spontaneous the organization is and on how much credit you've accrued in your perception bank. I try to offer the kind of autonomy that gives lots of permission to begin with."

Joy Collelli is the Vice President of Admissions at Mercy College. Reflecting on what generates risk taking, she noted, "Steven Covey says it so well in his *Seven Habits of Highly Successful People*: 'Seek first to understand, then to be understood.' Rushed and pressured, it's difficult to give people the time it takes to be fully present and to hear their point of view, especially when it's different from yours. But ultimately there's no choice here. My success is their success, and my people won't succeed without my patience and understanding. I try to have each of my managers convey this promise. I know the trust starts at the top: if we in charge can demonstrate patience and acceptance, it will flow all the way down."

Bruce Barkis, Marketing Manager at J.D. Powers, is very relieved to be in a situation where the fierce competition to produce numbers and please the boss does not feel like life and death, as it did in previous jobs. Bruce sees the use of personal style assessments like the Myers-Briggs or Wilson Learning's four social styles (discussed in the next chapter) as a means of generating respect. Seeing differences in this objective way helps him manage the respect and appreciation of differences. "Valuing diversity is about learning how differences add value to the team and workplace." Bruce explains. "My goal in using style instruments in trust and team building, is to articulate the concept of 'I like you because of our differences.' Defenses lower when everyone sees one another's styles and has a few laughs about strengths and vulnerabilities. Taboo subjects such as perceptions of first impressions and images are non-threatening, helpful, and friend-making activities after a while."

Barkis's discussion of style assessment tools reflects his belief in the importance of openness, risk taking, and vulnerability for the health of an organization. This non-defensive give-and-take about one another's reactions to differences in style, pace, and non-verbals helps clarify misconceptions and pushes beyond tolerance to acceptance of and, ultimately, learning from one anothers differences.

MUTUALITY AND SHARING

Trusting relationships are reciprocal. Among human beings, a kind of silent bargaining generally takes place to even the score. In business, for example, workers generally assess the level of fairness and evenness in their environment and find ways of leveling off their work output to match their perceived compensation.

For years, Marcia Worthing was Senior Vice President of Human Resources at Avon, and is currently spearheading a new set of services at an outplacement and executive coaching consulting firm, Mullin and Associates/Lincolnshire. There, as an Executive Vice President, she is focused on tailoring leadership and career development services to an overlooked yet growing segment of "workforce 2000:" women and people of color.

"Taking responsibility," says Worthing, "has to be the key ingredient in interpersonal and organizational trust. Taking responsibility is the opposite of blaming others. Trust builds when people have the grace and courage to take ownership of the conflicts and dilemmas of which they are a part. This is particularly true when it comes to managing and leading people. Even if a person is clearly wrong for the job, the supervisor who did the hiring, developing, performance managing, and coaching had a major role in that loss and failure. Supervisors don't often admit their part in that situation, losing a little trust and a lot of learning. If we could all admit to our part in all such human interactions there would be a lot more trust, a lot more productivity, efficiency and satisfaction."

Mutuality implies teamwork and reciprocity as well as taking responsibility, and I particularly like what Gerri Cevetillo has to say about being an active team player. Gerri is Vice President at Ultronics and Consumer Products Corporation, headquartered in Rockland County, New York. Having been in the business for over twenty years, she has seen a lot of changes in organizations and in the workforce. "I recapture or gain trust by keeping my ego in check, being a team player, and not cheating the company or my coworkers. It seems to start with the ego. If you feel superior or entitled, you'll do things to erode others' trust in you. You'll start to bend the rules, ask for and take more than what you are allowed, and take shots at your fellow employees. I keep my ego in check by remembering that there is a lot of good talent out there, and I, just like everyone here, am not indispensable. I have to write a purchase order for paper clips just as everyone else must. It's the little things that add up to a mountain when you're dealing with the precarious nature of trust."

TASK-RELATED COMPETENCE

Among the loudest cries of agreement I ever hear are the ones that come when I ask for a show of hands responding to the question, "Who here is now working for, or has in the past worked for, a clueless and incompetent supervisor?"

Now, you and I know that not <u>everyone</u> is so inept; the answer must lie within the trust factor. I believe perceptions of competence are related to perceptions of trustworthiness.

If you want to be perceived as more competent, share your motives for your behavior. Trust increases with increased understanding of why someone has chosen a course of action. Unknown motives combined with failure to inspire trust lead to limitless suspicion.

In order to trust, one has to have faith in the other party's capability in performing the behavior which you are hoping for or expecting.

"*Last man down, hatch secured!* are the sacred words uttered just before a submarine dives…Nothing is more important than trust aboard a sub." That's Mark Mula again, who understands trust from a unique point of view, having been a U.S. Navy submarine officer. "The lessons I learned about trust aboard ship—faith in a sailor's 'intent' to keep his promise as well as his 'competency'—have been immeasurably useful in civilian corporate life. Strengthening the culture of trust throughout [Warburg Dillon Reed Swiss Bank] worldwide is my unyielding personal and professional mission."

Most people answer in the affirmative when I ask, "Who here thinks that the Peter Principle applies: that organizations tend to promote people to their level of incompetence?" While such perceptions are influenced by dislike and distrust, upon probing, I discover some indisputable evidence.

Supervisors and managers tend to want to be surrounded by people they like. Given a choice between likability and competence, it seems that these folks' competence gauge becomes rather lenient. To the degree that organizations accept this practice, employees will feel justifiable resentment towards management and, if not among the favorites, reflect proportional disloyalty.

Katalin Polgar, Ph.D., is a medical researcher who has worked in three countries, in each of which, the relationship of effort and merit to promotion is different: Hungary, Italy, and the United States. "Having lived and worked in each of these countries, I have a good feel for the effect that favoritism has on productivity," she says. "Though never as politically repressive nor as passively compliant as the other so-called Communist bloc countries due to its strong Western alliances and blood-ties, Hungary was, nevertheless, Party-oriented, and your promotions in certain segments were dependent on being a Communist Party member in good standing. In Italy, family ties and personal relationships are so uniquely strong that promotions and other organizational relationships are shaped accordingly. Of the three, the U.S., as it advertises, is a land of opportunity relatively free of nepotism. It must be human nature, but here, too, in the U.S. there is some 'it's whom you know; not what you know,' but not anything like what I've known. Maybe that's why people here are so outraged by favoritism. Whenever it occurs, people get angry and lose respect and trust. Such behaviors are both common and accepted in Europe in general. We may tease our American cousins, but I (and many other Europeans) respect Americans' relentless and quite often, non-hypocritical efforts in business and also their general ethics."

INTERPERSONAL SENSITIVITY

Don't you hate it...

- When people call up and launch into their story/request/whatever, without once inquiring whether this is an OK moment for you?

- Or when people are so involved in themselves that you feel invisible around them—as if they could be talking to anyone, with no connection to anyone else's uniqueness?

- Or when people tell an off-color joke and are incapable of reading your expression of disgust, elbowing you to "get it" and laugh?

Interpersonal trust requires a sensitivity to feelings, your own and others'. No one will trust you if you don't show concern for them, their time, and their self-esteem. You can increase this interpersonal trust factor by simply inquiring about these concerns. "Would this be a good time to talk about that disagreement we were having?" and, "my intent in this conversation is to leave on a good note and to hear you out, not to punish you," are two excellent ways to reinforce trust.

Larry Tilley is a former superintendent of schools and college professor, and is currently an organizational development consultant and personal growth trainer. As you may recall, he was the leader of my first face-to-face communications laboratory and was, at the time, an instructor at the University of Connecticut. Larry has a lot to say about the word "trust" and its relationship to emotional maturity. Impressed by Goleman's work on Emotional Intelligence (EQ), he views EQ, like trust, as a function of personal awareness and interpersonal sensitivity. All of us who have worked with and studied under Dr. Tilley know his quip, "It takes two to know one." By this he means that a person must get feedback on the impact of his or her behavior on others. Only by seeing and understanding the impact of our words and behaviors on others and knowing where we stand with each other, can we modify those behaviors to continually improve our relationships with others.

"The only chance you have to establish or recapture trust," laments Alexander Lowen, the founder of Bioenergetics, "is to get close up, see, and look deeply into the individual, demonstrating in every way possible that you empathize with his or her feelings. You must also be able to experience and thus relate to your own feelings as you connect to the other on a feeling level. Should you then offer your reactions or advice as a supervisor, you may at least have the other more likely trust your intent."

Lowen asked me: "How can one even begin to trust others if they don't trust themselves? We know trust," he argued, "only when we know our feelings. When we *like* (a feeling) and *feel safe* (a feeling) and sense that a person feels our feelings, then we know trust. For example, when people appear to really understand our *fear* or *sorrow* (more feelings), we are more likely to trust them. But so many people are shut off from the neck down. Feelings are sensed in the body. Trust is sensed in the body. I guess," he sighed, "if you wish to recapture the trust in organizations (I don't believe there is that much to begin with, especially today), you would have to really get close to someone, let them know you understand them, reflect the deep feelings you sense they have but probably can't feel or acknowledge."

Now, if we look at trust from an organizational perspective, the workplace should be seen as an environment where information is shared freely, where mutual expectations are discussed and agreements kept, where unnecessary micromanagement and controls are nonexistent, and where people are not afraid to tell the truth and to "be themselves."

Julie Casella and consultant Lynn Diamond are tracking years of data at Chase Manhattan Bank that demonstrate that "trust is a function of interpersonal maturity." They see "maturity" in terms of ever-increasing self-awareness and self-confidence resulting in heightened sensitivity to the betterment of others. Julie concludes, "When people feel validated, they validate others, and we can all bring out the best in one another in a mutual learning environment." The learning in this case, Diamond and Casella argue, "Is first in personal growth, followed by intellectual growth. Corporate America has too long neglected the personal and the ego."

Marilyn Zavidow, Northeast Unit Marketing Director of William M. Mercer, makes unending efforts to have her staff feel equal to her in every way. This approach, she believes fosters a less stressful, more productive, and psychologically free climate that maximizes creative risk taking.

As part of the majority of working Americans today who spend most of their day at work, Marilyn makes sure work is a complete human experience that includes elements of belonging and meaningful creativity. She finds countless events to cherish and memorialize and creates office celebrations. Marilyn makes up songs and poems for everybody's birthday and for other special occasions and accomplishments in their lives. I've never seen a more upbeat and productive professional staff.

However, let's not be too naive. There are dangers. Some peo-ple are unwilling to trust or incapable of trusting behavior, and we must be on the alert to that possibility. While I do take the stand that trusting behavior begets trusting behavior and that in most circumstances, it's worth the risk of making that first trusting move, there are exceptions. Remembering that "organizational behavior" is a function of "culture," "rewards," and "personality," we need to ask ourselves:

- Does the "system" or "organizational culture" within which this interaction is taking place foster trusting behavior or suspicious, gamelike behavior?

- Does the system reward competitive or collaborative behaviors?

- Is there a two-way system of communication? Do managers, for example, get reviews from their employees? Do they ask for employee input before making decisions?

Leaders have both an extraordinary opportunity and responsibility to manage the culture of their organizations.

Joyce Newman, founder and President of The Newman Group, a New York City-based media and presentation skills training and consulting firm, is in the business of ensuring that leaders establish norms that have a positive impact on the attitudes, behaviors, and performance of their subordinates. She works on both content and style to reinforce trusting relationships, so that the listeners can believe both the "word and deed" of the speaker. The head of an organization has a profound impact on trust throughout the organization, as the next in line tends to follow the tone that is set from above. The importance of the delivery from the top is paramount...at each presentation!

"Our coaching helps leaders tap into their natural and unique style to communicate clear, efficient and articulate messages. Once leaders learn to trust this natural style they can model a dedicated work ethic, or a passion for a certain new product or service. Combined with a respectful way of interacting with others, the leader's passion and work ethic will be quickly internalized by others." However, Joyce cautions that the opposite is also true, reinforcing the importance of clear messages, both in content and delivery: "Without the ability to appropriately convey these desirable attitudes and behaviors, followers may either not get the message or, even worse, get the wrong message and proceed in a direction that is contrary to what the leader originally intended."

4
RECAPTURING THE TRUST

Thus far, I've examined the nature of trust from a personal and historical perspective, tracing the factors leading to a decline in organizational trust during the past half-century and demonstrating how easily trust can be eroded in the everyday working environment. I have included the thoughts and insights of people "on the front lines," who deal with matters of trust on a day-to-day basis, and whose viewpoint provides a measure of hope and inspiration.

In case you've been wondering where you fit into the equation, it all comes together right here, in this chapter. You'll take a look at what leaders and plain folks can do to enable the "functional behaviors" and reverse the decline in organizational trust. And you'll learn the techniques you can use to develop trust and to be a master communicator.

FORCES IN HUMAN BEHAVIOR AT WORK

Before a leader can begin to choose among the many techniques for recapturing the trust among his or her people, it is essential to have a basic understanding of the factors that affect human behavior at work.

People are the way they are in businesses and institutions largely because of their "personality" and how it meshes with organizational norms and rewards. This chapter will look at the major factors that affect personality, along with ways in which you can work with these factors and our system of organizational norms and rewards to maximize organizational trust and performance.

Personality

Why are there so many different types of people? How is it that two kids from the same family turn out so different? Why are some people open, others private; some fuzzy, others prickly; some playful, others solemn; some free spirits, others constrained; some trusting, others suspicious? To find out why, here is a basic primer in the psychology of human behavior as it relates to organizational behavior and human motivation. For simplicity's and brevity's sake, I've limited this discussion to the work of Sigmund Freud, Carl Jung, and Erik Erikson that, in my experience, best helps us to understand the complexities of human behavior at work.

Freud argued that our personalities are formed by two major influences: basic human instincts and our early family relationships. Freud believed that we are born with certain "drives" or "instincts," which he associated with that part of the mind he called the <u>id</u>, the source of our erotic and violent impulses. These instincts, he claimed, are acted on by our social conditioning (either parents or religious, community, and educational institutions) to form another part of our mind, the <u>super-ego</u>, or moral conscience. Id impulses aren't limited to sex and violence; they can be modified to include a host of behaviors seen in organizational life today. Think of the constellation of behaviors that takes place in daily work stemming from the id's evil shipmates, the traditional Seven Deadly Sins: pride, gluttony, greed, lust, envy, wrath, and sloth. When we feel these id-like emotions, our superego voices are appalled and cluck their tongues well before their external counterparts—colleagues and bosses—lay blame and shame, real or imagined. Finally, Freud named that part of the mind that deals with reality and always tries to find a negotiated settlement between the id, the superego, and external reality: the ego, or the mature self.

Defense Mechanisms

In order to maintain our ego as Freud defined it—our mature, respectable self unencumbered by childish impulses or critical parental attitudes—we employ certain defense mechanisms (behavioral strategies that enable us to protect our self-image). Defense mechanisms are a little like eating and drinking: they're OK in moderation. A modest amount of defensiveness is actually essential for mental health. Some people, however, carry defense mechanisms too far. We've seen them often enough, and understandably it's difficult to trust people who too frequently exhibit the defensive behaviors: rationalization, denial and projection.

"Oh, come on, everybody pads their expense accounts. They'll never know."

That's rationalization—constructing reasonable-sounding defenses of behaviors that we're irrationally committed to.

"Me, aggressive? Why you don't know what aggressive is until you've been to where I come from." Then you hear the same story you've heard far too often, while this individual still refuses to hear or accept your feedback about his or her aggressive behavior.

That's <u>denial</u>—refusing to consciously recognize a personal problem or shortcoming.

"Jerks! I'd like to swerve right into them so they'll flip over and smash into the guardrail. Can you believe the level of road rage out there?"

That's a clear case of <u>projection</u>—attributing one's own emotions to other people.

Most of us have a fairly well developed superego (conscience).
The more saint-like among us rarely use unconscious defenses because a highly developed empathetic regard for others tends to motivate their behavior. A small number of us, though, have a minimally developed conscience and may commit purposeful anti-social and exploitative acts often associated with the "psychopathic personality."

According to Paul Babiak, a Director of Human Resources at Ciba-Geigy Corporation (now part of Novartis), only the multiple screening processes in most rational organizations limit the entry of psychopaths into American corporations. "How-ever," he warns, "one in a hundred does sneak by, and once they do, they tend to advance quickly in the organization, leaving behind a swath of injured coworkers. They feign friendship and promise introductions and get-rich-quick deals that are too good to be true. Their cover is often protected, due to the shame felt by the spurned colleague, reluctant to admit his or her vulnerability to the false seduction. Due to this maneuvering, the organizational psychopaths can constitute some one in ten executives at the highest levels of American organizations." Babiak comforts us, however, with the premise that there are sufficient safeguards at these top levels so that, "While the psychopath may be capable of wreaking havoc, his or her destructiveness is kept in check."

There are other types of abnormal behavior as well. But my work is to help recapture the trust, not frighten it away. And the truth is that the really sick people are usually discovered before they enter most organizational systems or early in the process choose not to join such institutions. A few do get through, though, and cause a lot of damage and pain. We mildly dysfunctional types need to be able to ascertain these truly dysfunctional behaviors and deal with them accordingly.

To distinguish between human fallibility and outright psychological dysfunction, a supervisor need focus only on substandard performance. You needn't diagnose psychopathy or schizo-phrenia; just keep track of specific performance against clearly articulated standards. Recommendations to Employee Assistance Programs or other psychiatric referrals can be made after a person has been dismissed simply on performance criteria.

Freud also promoted the idea that our early family dynamics, that is, the relationships we had with our most intimate family members, usually mother, father, and siblings, also shape our adult behavior. Unhappy, untrusting, and conflict-burdened relationships with these early family members, if unresolved, tend to follow us all of our lives, popping up in look-alike situations. Freud called this repetition compulsion, meaning that people tend to unconsciously form relationships that repeat the patterns of earlier unresolved unhappy relationships in their childhoods. Until this problem is faced squarely, either with the family member himself or symbolically, through psychoanalysis, it will continue with other significant love and work figures.

Freud's work was about helping people uncover the unconscious effects of their unresolved early family dynamics on their present life. Someone still struggling with his or her independence from the parents or primary caretakers, where the struggle appears to be a continuous competitive battle with the same-sex parent and a concurrent over-attachment to the opposite-sex parent, might be analyzed as being stuck in the Oedipal stage. This, the most common of Freud's "stuck" places, may account for the "chip on the shoulder" of some employees who seem to continually get into difficulties and conflicts with all authorities. This kind of repetition compulsion plays out in the following way: an individual observes the behavior of another and will see an otherwise neutral action as "harmful." Misperceiving the intent of the other's behavior as negative, the individual then experiences hurt and anger. Typically, the hurt individual hurls some misguided retaliation, and a counter-punch by the other party leads to a vicious cycle that further distorts the truth and deepens the mistrust. Freud here shows us one very common unconscious psychological mechanism in which distrust between people is caused or at least exacerbated by an event lingering in someone's emotional memory, however dimly recalled, totally forgotten, and/or repressed.

Know any people whose behavior seems to fit the above description? Of course you do. And at times you see it in yourself, although, because it is unconscious to most of us most of the time, it's difficult to see it in our own reactions and behavior.

The goal of Freudian psychoanalysis is to "make the unconscious conscious," that is, to make the patient aware of the repressed emotions causing negative behavior patterns in order to be set free of them. If a person can see that many of his or her dysfunctional behaviors are the function of misplaced emotions, then he or she is less likely to act on those blind distorted impulses and more likely to see them for what they are: old responses or emotional overreaction. And having made this distinction, he or she may well choose to think about the reactions or even to rationally discuss the moment/situation.

How does the workplace reinforce these family dramas? According to Shoepf and Shoepf in *The Organization as Addiction*, the typical organization both attracts people from dysfunctional families and maintains the dysfunctional dynamic. The authors refer to the presence of the authoritative, punitive, unapproachable, and unassailable parent figure (boss) controlling the behaviors and frustrating the needs of a dependent oversolicitous child (employee). Because of a variety of unmet psychological needs exacerbated by addiction (drugs, alcohol, power, money, work), the child/employee's yearning for love/recognition continues the cycle of dysfunction.

To safeguard against the insidious effect of this dysfunctional behavior, you must use psychology in the workplace. If you treat people as adults, they'll respond in kind. "I shall always be a flower girl to Professor Higgins because he treats me as a flower girl and always will." This line from Lerner and Lowe's *My Fair Lady*, based, as you probably know, on George Bernard Shaw's *Pygmalion*, led Harvard social psychologist Robert Rosenthal to coin the phrase "The Pygmalion Effect," to convey the idea that people who are dependent on the evaluation of another will tend to define and measure themselves on the basis of how their supervisors define and measure them. People act in accordance with their self-image: erode their self-esteem, and you contribute to having them see themselves as weak and ineffective; treat them with dignity and respect, and you bring out their best. See them as independent and competent, and they will tend to act more independently and competently.

We can't discuss personality in a book about trust without noting the works of Erik Erikson. Erikson postulated that there are seven stages to a human's life, beginning with a trust/mistrust continuum at the beginning of one's life and concluding with a continuum of generativity/despair at its end. Putting trust first and foremost, he suggested that early childhood experiences will determine someone's level of trust in the world. This level of trust will then affect the rest of that person's life and each of its subsequent stages, culminating in a later adult life that may be characterized either by generativity (optimism, involvement) or by acceding to despair (pessimism, isolation). According to Erikson's findings, trust is an essential element of human well-being.

BEING A MASTER COMMUNICATOR

Using Psychology to Intervene in the Workplace

I'm often asked, "Do good leaders have to be psychologists too?" My answer is usually, yes and no. Yes, if you are defining a psychologist as someone who tells another his or her reactions in a concerned and diplomatic, yet direct, way. No, if the definition includes any kind of power differential, even for the sake of the other. You don't need me to tell you how defensive people can get when someone plays "know-it-all" and "This is what's good for you," with an attitude that "I'm OK and you're not." Yes, someone addressed in this way may appear to respond positively and carry out some order, but on only four of his or her eight cylinders; the other four are preoccupied with the insult of being treated without respect.

Instead of the word "psychologist," a more accurate descriptor for a manager with significant interpersonal skills is "master communicator." A master communicator can make the people with whom he or she interacts feel at ease, visible and important. The best leaders—speakers, mentors, coaches, and supervisors—have this kind of charisma. They can offer feedback and critique others in such a way that they feel grateful to hear it and, conversely, graciously listen to another's feedback and critique so that the person feels free to offer it.

How do you cultivate this mastery? In addition to being sensitive to the general psychological issues described previously, you can use two additional tools: "yourself as interpersonal barometer" and any of a variety of well-documented and researched personal style assessments. These two tools are used to help develop more openness and trust between people. The Johari Window, named for its creators, Joseph Luft and Harry Ingram (and sometimes even referred to as the "Joe-Harry" window), is a model that shows the amount of openness existing between people in any social context.

As you can see from Figure 1, the Johari Window is divided into four areas. The "open" area consists of "things I know about me and others know about me;" the "blind" area consists of "things I don't know about me but others do know about me;" the "hidden" area consists of "things I know about me but others don't;" and finally, the "unknown" area includes the "things about myself which no one knows."

The goal of trust and face-to-face communications training is to open the Johari Window, as in Figure 2, so that the open area becomes larger.

We do this by diminishing the other areas through the giving and receiving of feedback: the more I tell you about my reactions, thoughts, and feelings toward you, the smaller my hidden area; the more you tell me of your reactions to me, the smaller my blind spot. Notice that this reduction of hidden and blind areas also reduces the "unknown" area. This surfacing of a host of aspects of yourself that were hidden in the previous more restricted Johari condition is a side benefit of such exposure.

By becoming more in touch with previously unknown aspects of

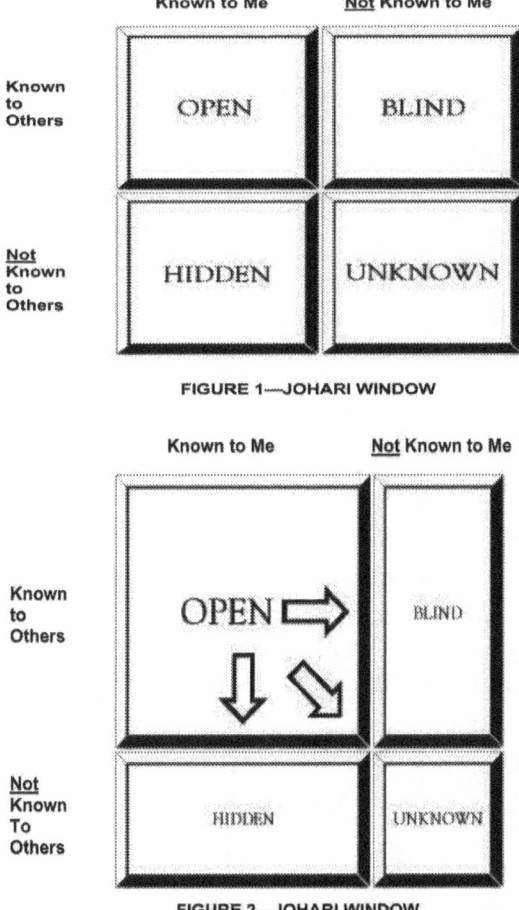

Known to Me   Not Known to Me

Known
to
Others

OPEN   BLIND

Not
Known
to
Others

HIDDEN   UNKNOWN

FIGURE 1—JOHARI WINDOW

Known to Me   Not Known to Me

Known
to
Others

OPEN ⇒   BLIND

Not
Known
To
Others

HIDDEN   UNKNOWN

FIGURE 2—JOHARI WINDOW

yourself and responses to others, you can enhance your inter-personal skills in the workplace and operate as an <u>interpersonal barometer</u>. Barometric readings tell about present and impending weather conditions; readings of your own "inner weather" (feelings, thoughts) can guide you more smoothly and suc-cessfully through the sometimes volatile conditions of interpersonal relationships.

Most people aren't aware of their personal reaction to others. When I ask people to describe their first impressions of, or reactions to, others whom they meet for the first time in one of my classes or workshops, few have distinct feelings that they can articulate. After a series of interpersonal and group classes, however, these same people are capable of sensing and expressing both their early and their subsequent emotional reactions toward one another's style/image and behavior. So I know that everyone is capable of being an interpersonal barometer.

Once you become mindful of the interpersonal moment, you receive an array of significant visual and auditory cues: postures, vocal tones, grooming, and body language. Each of these cues can, in turn, trigger reactions in you to use as data to help you find appropriate ways of dealing with individuals. Pay attention to what you may be feeling or sensing. Reactions such as "confusion," "shock," "intimidation," "pressure to agree," or "boredom" are all data points to consider in the evolving interpersonal picture.

In addition to your own cultivated personal sense of another, you can benefit from one or more of several popular personal style inventories. To give you a quick taste of these, here are the highlights of my current favorites, the FIRO-B, the Myers-Briggs, and Alessandra's "Platinum Rule."

Because of my early involvement with face-to-face communications laboratories, I've found the work of Bill Schutz, an early T-group pioneer, and his FIRO-B especially valuable. FIRO-B is an acronym that stands for Fundamental Interpersonal Relations Orientation Behavior. This assessment focuses on three dimensions related to our relationships with others, which he saw unfold so clearly in the T-group process: inclusion, control, and affection—Do we wish to be "in" or "out," would we prefer to be "up" or "down," is our desire to be "close" or "distant." The FIRO-B helps examine how these needs are expressed or lacking in one's life or work. And by comparing your scores with those of another, you can better anticipate (or at least make a better educated guess about) an incompatibility and adjust accordingly.

Probably the best known of the personal style profiles is the Myers-Briggs, which is based on the personality characteristics originated by Carl Jung, the famous Swiss psychologist and contemporary of Sigmund Freud. Jung disagreed with many of Freud's theories and saw personality as a function of lifelong choices, partly genetic and partly induced by socialization, that constitute a person's "type." The types for which Myers-Briggs tests, run along the following four dimensions: extrovert/introvert, sensor/intuitor, thinker/feeler, and judger/perceiver. Each of these character types involves a host of associated attitudes and behaviors, and certain combinations of them describe very recognizable and predictable patterns of behavior. The Myers-Briggs personality indicators are supported by an enormous amount of empirical research, and the results have been translated by practitioners into easy-to-read profiles of likely behaviors that most test-takers view as remarkably accurate.

To complement the Myers-Briggs, I like the four-style model and instrument taught by the Wilson Learning Corporation: amiable, expressive, analytical, and driver. A more recent contribution to the four-quadrant field of instrument devices is Tony Alessandra's "Platinum Rule," which identifies the relater, the socializer, the thinker, and the director.

How many times have others felt that you were acting in purposeful contradiction to a request they had made, when you were actually motivated by factors having nothing to do with them? And how many times have you mistakenly felt this way about others? More times than you may realize! Any of the personal style inventories—the FIRO-B, the Myers-Briggs or the Platinum Rule—has two purposes. The first is to help you understand why people see your behavior differently from the way you see it or from the way you intended to convey it; the second is to help you develop an appreciation of different innate personal styles—the diversity of ways that others have of seeing the world.

These formal style assessments are among many well-documented and successfully used instruments to help people further their mastery of interpersonal communications for any number of work and non-work related situations. For the most part, a keen sensitivity to the situation, awareness of your emotional reactions to another in the moment, and a comfort with one or more of the personal style instruments will give you the data you need to best size up an interpersonal problem situation.

The final component of masterful communication is the timing and words you use to deliver your message.

What, then, is the best way to correct poor behavior or performance? When someone does or says something that arouses a negative reaction or some significant disconnect in you, simply report your reaction calmly and respectfully to him or her right away, so as not to let the feeling fester and worsen. Factor in all you may know about the personal style profile of the individual and present your up-front statement of wishing to express your feelings toward this person and wanting to get back on track. This disclaimer will lessen the likelihood of a defensive reaction stemming from a predisposition to distrust.

That's it. That's the only psychological intervention you need to help someone get unstuck (at least temporarily) from his or her unconscious defensive reactions. Or, perhaps, in that gracious moment when you have earnestly asked for the same sort of feedback, you may become aware of something that you have unconsciously communicated. Either way, the best antidote to "Freudian craziness" is to practice the wonderful skills of telling the truth: the giving and receiving of feedback.

Dealing With Defensive Behaviors

Now I'm not suggesting that you put yourself at risk with someone who has shown that he or she may use your open, direct expression of perceptions and feelings for ulterior, destructive purposes. Don't open your Johari Window to lunatics, organizational psychopaths, or people so defensive that all statements get spun into hostile aspersions against them. Nor would you want to open your Johari Window to someone who is so politically motivated that he or she will use any confidences or information that you share against you. British actor Robert Newton's portrayal of Long John Silver, in the movie *Treasure Island* (1950), offers a classic example of the consummate con man and organizational psychopath, with the ship and its crew as the organization. Silver preys on his fellow pirates' greed to extricate himself from every hangman's noose, ceaselessly turning the tables on his less cunning cohorts. (Playing the role of subordinate coconspirator is a very dangerous move; the subordinate accomplice is always betrayed in the end.)

In today's less than healthy interpersonal environments, organizational citizens need to study the norms and the behaviors of others with regard to those norms. For example, when you find out, by gently testing the waters, that someone at work is not playing by the rules and is untrustworthy, you have one of several choices, depending on that person's position.

If it's a supervisor with whom you must interact, you can acquiesce to all unreasonable requests, as most, unfortunately, do. Or you can leave the organization—not a great or realistic alternative if you need the job. Or you can pretend to acquiesce, while manipulating things behind the scenes, doing what you know to have been right, knowing that your supervisor has been too busy pushing you around and will surely not even check up on your superior decision.

For instance, I know of an insecure supervisor who intimidates his employees by humiliating them in front of anyone who may be around—usually visitors or uninvolved coworkers. We discovered this supervisor's trigger: he would not tolerate disagreement or confrontation and behaved abusively to ward it off. We found the answer: Just don't contradict him. Tell him what he wants to hear; he's far more concerned with the moment than with what you may do afterwards. Of course, this is a choice of last resort.

More often, when you are in disagreement with, unsure where you stand with, or feeling distrustful or alienated towards your boss, you can confront. Be careful, though; confronting a defensive or manipulative superior has its hazards. To accomplish this, the most frequently requested of all business skills, I recommend the following action steps, adapted from those designed by Dr. Bernard Rosenbaum, while he was serving as President of MOHR Development, Inc.):

Asking For Feedback From a Defensive Supervisor

- Determine a mutually convenient time to discuss a business/professional/personal matter.

- Start by allowing this person an "out." Avoid having him or her feel "cornered," that is, required to "give you feedback." Say something like, "Maybe it's in my head, J.B., but lately I've noticed..." This statement will allow your superior an opportunity to get off the hook by saying, "Yeah, it's all in your head, now scram."

- The point here is to alert this individual to your concern. Whether he or she wishes to acknowledge the issue at this moment is less important than the fact that the concern has been raised and will have an impact on your relationship. This may be as far as you can go. If you should have the misfortune of dealing with one of our "organizational psychopaths," this step can help you diagnose the degree of out-of-hand defensive or potentially manipulative reactions you might anticipate.

- While maintaining sensitivity to your supervisor's position and concerns, indicate that you can "take the heat" by getting to the point with specifics. Introduce your specifics by saying something like, "It's important that I fully understand and respond to your needs and expectations, so please let me know where I seem to be off-base. There are a couple of signs that tell me I've missed something."

- In a non-accusatory way, indicate wherein your perception or views of the problem situation differ from your supervisor's. The respectful confidence with which you deliver your presentation is important, since it could protect you from being seen and abused as the passive chicken type (the psychopath's basic diet) or as a subordinate coconspirator, as in my earlier "Long John Silver" example.

- After identifying your supervisor's behaviors and how you have interpreted them, check the validity of your perceptions and listen non-defensively to whatever reactions evolve.

- If confused about the specific behaviors and/or performance that may have aroused those perceptions, respectfully ask for specific instances, so that you may better work at changing these behaviors (should that be indicated).

- Misconceptions, disconnects and the like generally result from a combination of both parties' behaviors. It could therefore be useful if you were to identify and communicate to your supervisor, those behaviors that he or she might adopt to help you modify your performance: things that might be said or done to improve your relationship.

- Thank this person for the feedback, letting him or her know what you will do, by when, and how both of you will be able to recognize the value of this conversation.

That—confronting your superiors—is perhaps the most difficult of the touchy organizational communications techniques. Now let's turn to the second most frequently requested skill: dealing with working relationships at an equal level or with subordinates. These relationships involve a different set of risks and obstacles. To be successful in the workplace, you need to keep peers as allies as much as possible, and you need to maintain the loyalty, morale, and motivation of your staff.

Disappointments and disconnects are happening all the time at work. The sooner you approach these situations in a constructive way, the more trust you can build and maintain. In most situations, adapting the following strategy to your particular style and interpersonal performance structure, will elicit a favorable response from peers and subordinates.

Dealing with an Attitude or Performance Concern with a Peer or a Subordinate

- Determine a mutually convenient time to discuss a business/professional/personal matter.

- At the meeting, indicate your intent, your ultimate objective for the meeting; it should be to repair some misunderstanding or error, so that the air can be cleared and your working (or personal) relationship put back to "normal."

- Focus on the specific behavior (performance, skill, statement), indicating why it's a problem. Make it clear that you would like to hear your peer or subordinate's side of the issue and discuss it.

- Actively listen to his or her response, demonstrating your good will in hearing the reasons and letting the individual fully respond and feel "heard."

- Reasonably soon, focus on the "future" and what you both can do, so that the situation will improve.

- Write down and commit to those promises made by both of you, so that this and other similar events are less likely to occur in the future.

- Indicate your confidence in this individual's ability to honor these commitments. Set a follow-up date to note progress and/or completion.

TRUST-BUILDING FOR TEAMS

The concept of team playing is very American. It suggests a fairness where all players play by common rules and are punished by common penalties. Too often, teams have gotten a bad rap in organizations because, for political reasons, some people are able to play by different rules. Nobody likes favoritism. It erodes trust and breaks down the potentially great benefits of teamwork.

Team building is all about trust. Once trust is attained within a group, no one counts who has done more than whom. Teamwork suggests a belief in the synergy of the group: that more productivity, more creativity, more profit, more of anything we individuals want, will result from doing something together rather than doing it alone.

Team building consultant that I profess to be, I'm ashamed to admit that I (as most of my clients) dislike most teams. But that's because many teams are loathsome places. It's bad enough to be in a lifeless conversation with just one other; but in a group, ugh! It's torture to sit among ten or twelve egos jockeying for position as the most knowledgeable or most witty.

The best way to cultivate and reinforce trust and teamwork is to have the group "process" its relationships. Process, in this context means to "discuss the underlying relationship issues." Certain underlying relationship issues need to be presented to team or group members so that they may critique and evaluate their progress. This can be accomplished by having team mem-bers respond, using a scale of 1 to 10 (low to high), to a simple list of questions, which elicits an evaluation of the behaviors exhibited by the team:

- Was the session conducted in a spirit of trust and openness?

- Did participants demonstrate listening skills and empathy?

- Were all relevant players involved and did they participate?

- Were differences respected?

- Were roles and responsibilities clearly understood?

- Did Individuals feel a sense of belonging?

It's best to ask these questions after some team task, limiting the participants' responses to reactions about only their teamwork during this last task.

One very effective trust building tool is a group-on-group encounter model. This works well in situations where hostile and untrusting behaviors have gone on for some time. In this classic model, designed by Richard Beckhart, two opposing units (two classically mistrusting departments, for example) go to an offsite. A facilitator gives each group three blank sheets of newsprint, one entitled "what we think of us," the second, "what we think of them", and the third, "what we think they think of us." Encouraging each group to write its perceptions down in this way helps to reduce possible awkward timidity. It is astounding how little of this direct feedback occurs in organizations. In twenty-eight years of conducting this, the most poignant of trust-building exercises, I've never seen negative fallout, either immediate or long-term. (One caution, however: the qualified professional facilitator should know the culture, departments, and individuals sufficiently well to determine the boundaries of acceptable responses and the appropriate circumstances for timely interventions.)

Another team-building tool is the "strength bombardment," sometimes called a "validation exercise." It is an experience that leaves everyone buoyant and optimistic. It, like all human relations training, reinforces trust through authentic contact, self-disclosure, the clarifying of roles and expectations, the fostering of equality, and the suspension of the impersonal attitudes and behaviors that arise from status differences. Here's how it works:

In a group of three to no more than eight individuals, have each person think about each of the people in the group. These people may know one another for some time or not, just as long as they have had some exposure to one another, enough to have gathered some "first impression" intuitive data.

Have each in turn be on the "spot"—a happy spot, that is, because each of their counterparts will, one at a time, identify some specific thing he or she likes about the person: one specific thing that the person said or did that may have been enjoyed, appreciated or identified with and caused a good feeling about the person.

This technique can be used even among people who may be angry with or mistrustful of one another! The point is not to fake a liking, but rather to set aside, if necessary, any negative thoughts and enjoy that component of the other's behavior that is liked. The effect on group morale and individual joy is remarkable!

ORGANIZATIONAL NORMS AND REWARDS

Now that we've examined some of the reasons why people may behave or misbehave as a function of their given personalities, lets take a look at how organizational culture affects organizational behavior and trust among individuals.

Norms are the unwritten rules that most people are expected to follow in a specific culture or subculture. They exist at the "macro" and the "micro" level; that is, the overall organization and your department. To understand how norms develop, take a look at your immediate work situation, be it a staff, team, department, crew, unit, whatever. Levels of productivity, interpersonal trust, and satisfaction, are of course, influenced by individual personal factors, but these personal factors are also profoundly affected by norms.

One large overarching factor is the country in which you live, let's say the USA. Here, national norms call for fairly high levels of individuality, ambition, assertiveness and stoicism. A next level of norms might be determined by your region of the country. Forgive the stereotype, but, to make a point, the Northeast is often characterized as fast-paced and more distant to strangers, whereas the Southwest is characterized as slower-paced and more likely to acknowledge strangers.

Think about how these norms and values may affect the behaviors and expectations in your organization.

What impact may they have on the degree of trusting relationships?

Your organization's product or service and the status and size of your organization also affect interpersonal behavior. Consider the norms at play in the faculty at Harvard, Pepsico World Headquarters, the United Nations, an urban police precinct, a Wall Street law firm, a Silicon Valley chip shop, and a small men's clothing store. Harvard, for example, features the casual sweater, weathered briefcase, and hours spent on intellectual banter; Pepsico favors neat, formal, brief business-like conversations; and so forth, for each distinct entity.

The norms of your organization can also be determined by written policies and procedures. Human Resource Management comes out with reams of written documents reflecting life inside the organization. Both the content and the style with which these regulations are written reveal the organization's cultural norms. Policies can be expressed so that a little or a lot is left to the judgment of the employee. Wording can be expressed authoritatively or softly. Notice the difference in mood (and the level of your likely compliance), if a notice reads one of the following ways: "Any recording of this performance is strictly forbidden." vs. "Please do not record this performance, as this is our only way to protect our copyrighted material."

What are the norms at play in your organization?

A subsection of an organization's norms and policies is its reward system, both psychological and financial. Depending on the organization, both of these types of rewards can be forthcoming or rare, as people can be generous or stingy with their praise as well as their purse.

Noted psychologist, B.F. Skinner got us to realize that humans, like animals, behave in response to their reinforcers. Simply put: rewards get you more; punishment gets you less. Rewards like a heart-felt public thank you and/or a bonus tied to a specific project well done are powerful motivators.

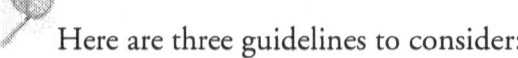 Here are three guidelines to consider:

- Recognize individual as well as team effort by dividing rewards for both. Depending on the organizational culture, the rewards can either be divided equally or divided with a larger share given to the bigger producers.

- There is a lot of variation in what people define as "rewarding." Know your people. Observe and ask!

- Be careful not to reward the same people over and over with a single bonus plan. Develop an incentive plan that recognizes effort and progress as well as bottom-line numbers.

5

FACE-TO-FACE
COMMUNICATIONS LABORATORIES

RECAPTURING THE TRUST...WITH THE ULTIMATE TRUST-TRAINING MACHINE!

Trust doesn't develop in a vacuum; it requires a conscious commitment by leaders and by organizations. A key stepping-stone to this commitment can be provided by a leadership training vehicle known as "face-to-face communications labora-tories."

Larry Tilley has, for nearly thirty-five years, trained thousands of individuals in the art of sensitivity training, known in the early days as the "T-group," a shortening of the phrase, "human relations training group." Initially, the T-group was designed for and delivered to high-level leaders to sharpen their ability to give and receive feedback, better understand group and team dynamics, and practice the emotional/interpersonal aspects of leadership. After some fifteen years of popularity among many industries, the T-group lost much of its following, which migrated to many of the emerging group therapies in the 'sixties.

There are, however, many of us who still use this basic human-relations model (often supplemented by the better-known "Rogerian encounter" techniques).

The face-to-face communications laboratory has emerged over the last thirty years as a powerful leadership-training tool, primarily because of its effectiveness in building and developing trust. Over this time, my colleagues and I have modified the training in order to keep pace with changing trends and needs.

The T-group and this updated variation are often cited as among the best management and leadership learning tools ever conceived. Unlike most small-group training used to reveal face-to-face and group dynamics phenomena, this method provides no structured exercises. Rather, face-to-face communications laboratories, by facilitating an accelerated learning and culture-forming environment, create a community or a team whose every dynamic (roles, feelings, power and politics, conflicts, competition, and levels of trust) can be seen and critiqued to the sometimes skeptical, sometimes astonished, and sometimes profoundly moved participants.

In a group of eight to twelve strangers (all selected from different organizations and preferably from richly diverse backgrounds), the two-day process calls for participants to express their spontaneous reactions to one another in the group. Com-munication in the group is limited to developing an "authentic" relationship with every person in the group. "Authentic" simply means "honest" and is based on the offering of feedback to another on the way you reacted to what he or she may have said or done during your time together. This act of offering your own reactions and asking for others' reactions to any and all the things you say and do is unusual in human interaction. Most of the time we keep such feelings to ourselves, act and converse in our own characteristic ways, follow conventional ways of acting and talking, and remain relatively unknown to one another, at least in terms of the impact we may have on one another.

The uniqueness and binding force of these laboratories lie in the experience of trust. The very act of giving and receiving feedback from others, positive or negative, is the foundation of interpersonal trust.

Awkward at first, each individual tries in his or her way to express honest reactions. As the trust builds, the give-and-take increases, participants begin to ask for the range of reactions to their behavior, and different personalities and roles begin to emerge. The pace soon becomes enlivened as the trust increases even more, and people learn to take the most rewarding risk one can take in the group: that of asking for feedback from those in the group they fear don't like them and/or from whom they feel most different and/or most distant. The willingness to give and receive negative and positive feedback is the most constructive trust-building skill that develops from the group process.

People feel respected when they know where they stand with one another. The security that comes from this respect allows a freer flow of feelings. With feelings more up front, conflicts and misunderstandings are also up front and easier to resolve and correct.

The leadership implications of this communications experience are enormous!

What a leadership learning experience it is, to see how conflict or strong difference of opinion can be managed in a respectful and caring way! Not only does this reinforce the observer's belief in the ultimate humanness that lies beneath the defensiveness, but it's living evidence that:

• Trustful human relations are possible in human systems.

• People can be emotionally honest with each other.

- People can like and respect each other, not only despite their differences, but also because of them.

- There is a deep need for contact in every human being.

Despite all the layers that appear to deny this, when people work at this level of contact and authenticity, the resulting joy is so overpowering and the resulting collaboration so intense, that there is no question of its profound impact on organizational productivity and commitment.

This is leadership training!

Well-trained facilitators, while they are equal members in the group (demonstrating how strong leadership can coexist with being an equal in human relations terms), ensure the emotional comfort and safety of group members by modeling the delicate skills of authentic feedback, facilitating participants' responses and intervening where necessary to help maintain a psychologically safe environment and pace.

The face-to-face communications laboratory evolves through stages identical to those of organizational teams, only more quickly and more obviously. Participants are encouraged to witness the stages as the group moves circuitously from guarded politeness to cautious disagreement to tentative understanding to deep respect, mutuality, and even liking...all in a period of hours.

These groups also provide a rare opportunity in which people can gather to practice the skills and experience the wonder of authentic relationships: finding out how others see them and taking the risk of revealing that which lies beneath their facades; knowing how others really feel about them and having that feel good, irrespective of the level of liking.

The One-Day Laboratory

For some people, the time, distance, and effort required for the two-day offsite is too much.

In response to these concerns, an alternative program for building trust and leadership skills, the <u>advanced face-to-face communications laboratory</u>, has been developed. Using a one-day format, at convenient locations, this streamlined process involves six to ten "strangers" from different organizations.

In order to have the group members get multiple glances at each other's personal and professional style, the morning session consists of several paired and group exercises designed to simulate scenarios from the work world, with a rule not to reveal one's educational and/or professional background. By noon, the highly anticipated feedback and critique session begins with a matching test, where participants try to figure out who's what. A discussion about why people may have thought one to be "the stock broker," another, "the college president," another, "the executive," launches the afternoon's work. During this session, each person finds out as much as possible about the impact and impressions that he or she may have made during the course of the day.

The combination of experienced facilitators and the gradual and appropriate self-disclosure deepens the trust, enabling individuals a rare opportunity to explore their most profound and anxiety-filled questions—a chance to ask the other members of the group: Would you buy my product from me? Would you hire me? How would you feel working for (or with) me?

Now everyone can get the amount of feedback he or she desires. The depth of the critique can be set by the participant, who expresses those issues, dilemmas, and questions he or she wishes to be addressed.

Subsequent day-long "stranger" workshops (Levels II and III) offer another set of communication and leadership skills. The feedback-and-critique sessions at these workshops enable a more sustained and deeper examination of oneself and one's impact on others, provide an additional opportunity to gain and practice the techniques that enhance personal and professional style, and help sharpen those skills so necessary for recapturing the trust.

6
CONCLUSION

Having read this far, you have probably trusted and accepted a number of my thoughts related to recapturing the trust in today's organizations. You've read about how others in situations just like yours have overcome obstacles and have made progress in recapturing the trust around them. You've assessed your supervisory and general organizational situations, and have evaluated some potential new ideas and behaviors.

While I believe that the human condition with respect to trust will remain fairly constant, I also know that the norms and conditions of organizational life will change enormously, affecting some of the norms concerning the etiquette of trust.

My mission is to stay current on both the organizational and relationship fronts, and I would like you to be part of my ongoing research and development. I would be eager to know your response to this book, your reactions to its tips and tools, the outcomes you have achieved and the results on the trust questionnaires. And should your situations be unique, or should you have a variation on the many themes outlined in this book, and you'd like to discuss that with me, you can reach me by mail at 30-D Putnam Green, Greenwich, CT 06830; by e-mail at **rschachat@worldnet.att.net**, or by phone at 203-531-0919. I will keep and process this data and post up-to-date statistics, implications, and recommendations on my website.

My website at www.robertschachat.com is devoted to the trust data and other follow-up information for readers of this book. There is a description of the various trust building services, including the locations and scheduling of the various face-to-face communication seminars.

I am excited about the business and technology changes that are zooming our way. The past decade has been a most astonishing and dramatic period, full of explosive developments. The phenomenal pace at which this "information age" is evolving will undoubtedly be for us what the industrial revolution was for those who knew nothing but a previous ten thousand-year history of agriculture.

What the industrial revolution's first two hundred years were like for our forebears, the next ten years will likely be for us.

I hope you will join me in stimulating trusting relationships in the places where we live and work.

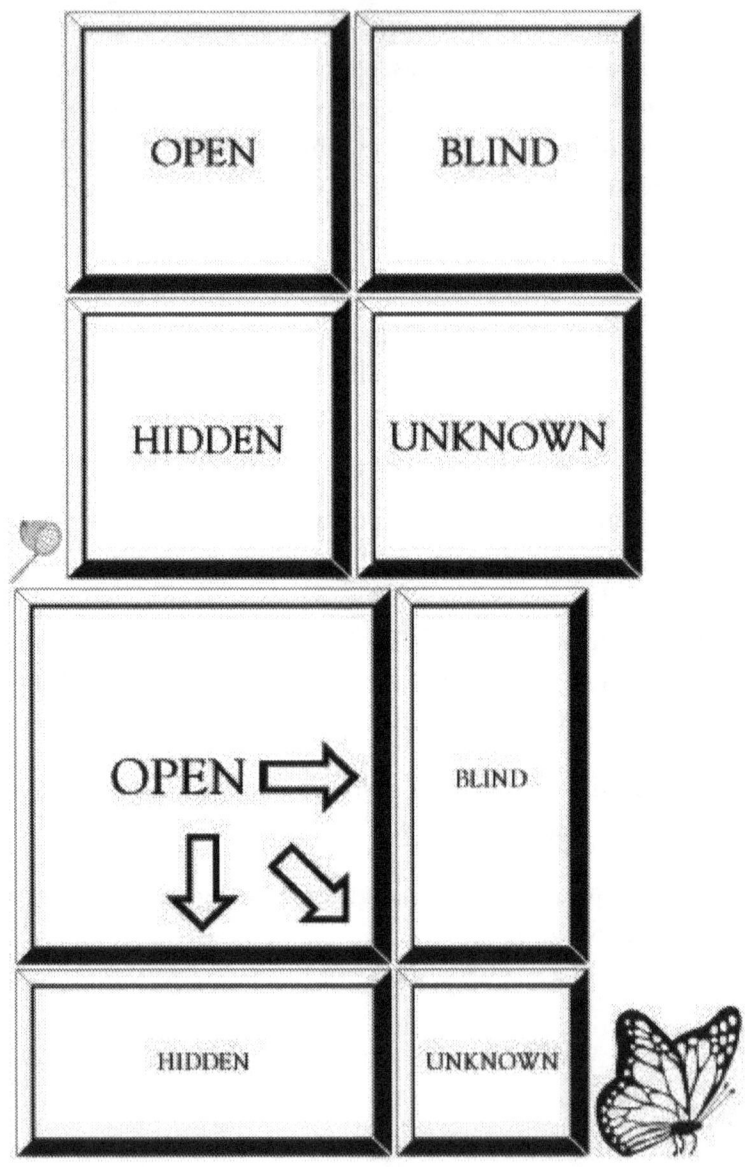

0-595-27882-5